WI

of Chinese Poetry

THE
SHAMBHALA ANTHOLOGY
of Chinese Poetry

Translated and edited by

J. P. SEATON

with additional translations by

James Cryer

Shambhala
Boston & London
2006

Shambhala Publications, Inc.
Horticultural Hall
300 Massachusetts Avenue
Boston, Massachusetts 02115
www.shambhala.com

9 8 7 6 5 4 3 2 1

First Edition
Printed in the United States of America

⊗ This edition is printed on acid-free paper that meets the American
National Standards Institute z39.48 Standard. Distributed in the
United States by Random House, Inc., and in Canada by Random
House of Canada Ltd

Interior design and composition: Greta D. Sibley & Associates

Library of Congress Cataloging-in-Publication Data

The Shambhala anthology of Chinese poetry/translated and edited
by J. P. Seaton.
p. cm.
Includes bibliographical references.
ISBN-13: 978-1-57062-862-7 (alk. paper)
ISBN-10: 1-57062-862-9
1. Chinese poetry—Translations into English. I. Title: Anthology of
Chinese poetry. II. Seaton, Jerome P.
PL2658.E3S43 2006
895.1'1008—dc22
2006000179

Dedication

THIS BOOK IS A "LIFE'S WORK." AS SUCH, IT IS DEDICATED to too many to name, who were just enough to keep me at it for forty years. Of my teachers, F. A. Bischoff, above all. Influences, and a joy to know, Carolyn Kizer and Ursula K. Le Guin, each of whom changed my life and my work. Fast friends: Bill Bollinger, Brad Langley, Jim Cryer, Jim Sanford: who could ask for more. Students, from 1968 until 2004, five or six thousand, twenty or thirty of whom should know for sure that I remember them. I *do*, and thank you here.

Finally though, this book is dedicated to Rosalie Katherine Paradiso Seaton and her three children, without whom this life would not have been lived nor this work ever begun. Everything begins in the family, or so the Chinese philosophize.

Contents

PART FOUR

A Few Strong Voices Still Singing
Poetry from the Sung (960–1279), Yuan (1279–1368),
        Ming (1368–1628), and Ch'ing (1644–1911)
        Dynasties to the Twentieth Century

Introduction

THIS INTRODUCTION WAS WRITTEN TO OFFER YOU SOME information about Chinese poetry and about the arrangement of the anthology, to help you to get started. It begins with a little discussion of the extremely elevated place of poetry in traditional Chinese culture. I then discuss as briefly as possible the nature of the writing system that makes Chinese poetry unique in world literature, and the interesting variety of poetic forms in which Chinese poets put their language to use. If I come close there to suggesting that Chinese poetry can't really be translated at all, you must try to remember that while poets (and translators) generally agree that "the translator is a traitor," as the Italians say, and "poetry is what is lost in translation," as Robert Frost said, the knightly translator in his chamber-pot helmet continues to create literature that can be read for learning and for pleasure, and that without the treacheries of my fellow translators you couldn't read Chaucer, much less Homer, Sappho, or Catullus. Next I dash through an introduction to the poets who have seemed to me for one or another reason most clearly worth singling out. Some of the poets left out of this introduction may appeal to you more than the "headliners" in the act, and you may feel free to regard my standouts as merely your landmarks as you wander through the book. Finally, inspired by a reencounter with a poem by Li Po, I end with a sentimental cry for peace on earth and goodwill toward men, women, and children, and an invitation to begin reading poems.

In traditional Chinese culture, poetry held a place that was unrivaled by any other single talent, ability, or practical accomplishment as a source of prestige, affluence, and even political power. Literacy was a source of potency in all premodern societies, and literary prowess was and is admired and acknowledged as a gateway along the path of social mobility in many Western cultures (French, Italian, German, even English). However, nowhere else has it even approached the position it held in traditional China. The reason for its preeminence there lay directly in the many pronouncements of the Master Sage, Confucius, that linked together, under the Chinese term *wen*, a number of things that go beyond even the most advanced conception of literacy in the West.

Wen was to be acquired by a twofold process. Fundamentally, the word refers on the one hand to *decoration*, that which is applied to the outside of an object of sacred worship or of civil ritual, or to a cup, or a house, or a man or a woman. On the other hand, *wen* also refers to the patterns that occur and recur in nature: ripple patterns in the sand of a streambed, or the grain in the wood of a freshly cut board, always apparent in the raw wood but always more evident and more beautiful when rubbed and oiled and rubbed again, to glow with a warm sheen. So too, a man or a woman may decorate clothing, or even skin, to attract attention. So too, say the Confucians, one must rub and polish one's natural grain: the Confucian believes that human nature is good at birth and that it may, with care, glow with a warm sheen. To accomplish *wen* is, finally, in the simplest terms, to accomplish the ability to communicate fully and powerfully.

Wen includes the most advanced forms of passive literacy: reading with discernment, critically and analytically, and with a joyful appreciation of the aesthetics of the written word as well. Beyond these, *wen* is also active literacy at its most powerful. It is the ability to create through language, to communicate with passion and power. It includes not just the ability to argue brilliantly but also the ability to marshal beauty on the side of truth in the ultimate form of humane argument.

The five books that Confucius used in his teaching, what we call the Chinese Classics, included a poetry anthology, the *Shih Ching*. It is the largest of the five. These books, though they do not claim divine authority, were as influential in traditional Chinese culture as the Bible is in Christian societies or the Koran in Islamic. Using each of these books, Confucius taught that literacy granted the ability to cross the barriers of both time and space through the *study* of history and literature. Further, he taught that self-cultivation in the arts of *wen* gave the honest student (or scholar, as we in the West have called the traditional Chinese gentleman who followed the Master's injunctions) the tools to master the arts of communication.

And though a clean and clear prose style was an ideal of Confucius, *poetry* was the mode of communication par excellence. According to Confucius, the cultivated man, speaking through poetry, the most powerful literary medium, achieved Te, *charisma*, the almost magical power to lead the community in peace and even, when necessary, in war.

The vehicle that made all this powerful communication, all this world-ordering charisma, possible was itself unique, a one-of-a-kind written language, based in turn on a system of writing completely unlike any other in the world.

All Western languages are written using one or another form of alphabet: *letters* used to represent the *sounds* of spoken words. There are advantages to alphabetic writing. Once you learn a relatively small and clearly defined set of letters of your given alphabet, you can "sound out" any word in your own language, and if you know it by ear, you can also "read" it. But there are problems. The pronunciation of words changes over time, and so the farther away you are from a source text, say Shakespeare (who can be hard to read) or Chaucer (impossible without special training), the harder it gets to understand what you're reading, even in your own language. Also, language change is accelerated across national borders. So speakers of Italian, French, and Spanish, for instance, could understand each other's spoken language two thousand years ago, but they can't today. Thus we might say that alphabets cause us to grow apart from even the closest members of our human families, helping space and time to separate us.

Though it is not what most people find most immediately fascinating about the Chinese writing system, its most important feature is the fact that its characters carry meaning independent of sound. They carry pronunciation and meaning both, but the meaning of the characters stays the same, even as the inexorable laws of sound change make the pronunciations of all words in Chinese change at the same rate as do the words of Greek, Russian, Italian, or English.

Every single Chinese character represents a single spoken syllable. That syllable may be a single spoken word, or it may represent one part of a polysyllabic word. Chinese has never been, as so many well-intentioned authors have told us all, a monosyllabic language. There are in fact fewer one-syllable words in spoken Chinese than in spoken English. But since the Chinese writing system consists of single-syllable characters, each of which does have a meaning, any writer who wants to communicate the meaning of a two- or three-syllable spoken word with a single character can do so.

Economy, or elegance, as even a scientist routinely puts it, has almost always been regarded as a mark of superior literary style in every culture in the world. So it's not surprising that from the beginning, most Chinese authors have chosen to use one character to express the meaning, in writing, of polysyllabic spoken words: in addition to being a rule of good writing in most languages, *in the beginning,* when *the word* was out of necessity scratched or carved on relatively hard materials, it made extra good sense.

Maybe that's how it began: laziness as the mother of invention. But whatever the reason, long before most of the poems presented here were written, *most* written Chinese was as close to being monosyllabic as writers could make it. Within poems and prose pieces the drive toward verbal economy also set a premium on extreme grammatical simplicity. Spoken Chinese can be as joyously redundant and wordy as any medium of gossip in the world, but classical Chinese is positively telegraphic.

But now to the fascinating stuff!

The traditional Chinese characters fall into three basic categories: pictographs (which *sometimes* look delightfully, excitingly like what they mean), ideographs of two types (a few of which are among the most interesting elements in the language), and finally a somewhat complicated type (extremely important in artistic terms), the phonetic/signific compound.

The pictographs came first, certainly. They represent simple *things*: always the real, the phenomenal, never the imaginary or the abstract. When introduced to them and to the simpler of the ideographs by the first Jesuit China scholars, the great German polymath Gottfried Wilhelm Leibniz (1646–1716), a contemporary of Isaac Newton and inventor of calculus in the notation still used today, wondered if they might not be the perfect *language of phenomena*, the way to talk about everyday, bump-your-toe-on-it, "real" things, even as mathematics is the language of abstraction. Some of the characters easily reveal their meanings even to an untrained eye, and when we look at older, less stylized versions of these little pictures, as traditional Chinese poets always did in the process of learning, and in everyday life in traditional Chinese culture where they were used ceremonially, we can easily discern many, many *things*, from the sun and the moon to mother and baby, from mountain and river to fish and horse and bird. Fewer than 15 percent of the characters are pictographs, but when one appears in a line of poetry, it announces its presence directly to the right brain, where visual images are processed, as well as to the left brain, where *language* is processed. For a moment at least, the reader may perhaps experience the thing represented directly.

Words in alphabetic script enter the left brain as spoken words, without raising a flicker in the visual cortex.

The ideographs come in two types. The simple ideograph offers a picture of an idea, an abstraction. Beyond a surprisingly few extremely simple concepts, this is very hard to do, and there are very few. Simple horizontal lines piled on top of each other give us the first three numbers; after that, as the allowed standard space gets crowded, this gives out as a *method*. In another, a horizontal line meets a vertical at the top, with a little mark beside it apparently meant to say, "It's the direction of the vertical stroke that counts, stupid!," because the character indeed means "down, under, inferior," while a horizontal line met by a vertical line at the bottom, with the same wiseacre little dot beside it means "up, on top of, superior." After a few other stumbles, the earliest generations of character inventors gave up on the "simple" ideographs. So we can say that the characters are not particularly good at rendering abstractions. We can agree with Leibniz that perhaps math is the better alternative here. On the other hand, the Chinese have no trouble with abstractions or abstract words in their thought or in their spoken language, nor do they have trouble rendering spoken words created to express abstractions into quite understandable characters.

After the simple ideographs came compound ideographs, and these were much more successful. They are characters constructed by juxtaposing (side by side or in some close physical relationship) two or more *preexisting* pictorial elements. Two trees placed side by side make a grove, and three (for design's sake, two below and one above) make a forest. A sun beside a moon means "bright." A woman beside a child means, interestingly, "good" or, more interestingly, "addicted" or "passionately dependent." A human being beside the number two indicates a more abstracted sort of goodness: "benevolence" or "compassion," a philosopher's term to stand beside the visceral good that are woman and child, to any eye but a fear-crazed soldier or a cold-hearted dictator. This more abstract word means "Good" or "Goodness" for Confucius and Confucians. It is that which we owe each other because we are human, all some mother's child. A poet like the powerful Sung poet, historian, political magnate, and literary patron Ou-yang Hsiu could shock his readers, Hemingway style, by using the former character, rather than any of a hundred more nuanced pieces of literary vocabulary for natural "goodness" or beauty, to describe a place and a state of mind it produced, while Confucian philosophers, under the influence of Taoist and Zen thought, would expand their meaning of the second "good" further, to say that any human facing any other *thing* must know love. A great green good, a tender love of all the world, the whole material universe, one thing at a time!

Between them, the two types of characters, pictographs and ideographs, constitute less than about 15 percent of the characters in the largest Chinese dictionary. The vast majority of the remaining characters are of the third type, what I will call (different folks have used different terminology) the phonetic/signific compounds. A phonetic/signific compound consists of one element that gives a clue—sometimes a very slight one, because language sounds change in time—to the pronunciation of the character, and another element that gives an often very general and sometimes downright indiscernible indication of the class of meaning into which the character falls. For many characters, however, the signific is powerful: almost every one of the hundred or so characters found in any Chinese-English dictionary that have the signific element *mountain* have something to do with mountains. A majority of the nearly nine hundred in the forty-volume complete Chinese-language dictionary do also. Almost every single character in that Chinese-English dictionary that contains the element *fish* is the name of a particular variety of aquatic life. Here the signific shouts, "It's a fish" at the beginning reader, while the phonetic says, "Try the words you know that sound something like me." But many "signific" elements are required to act in too many characters, thus leading to an ambiguity that makes them useful only as mnemonic devices, memory aids once the learner has memorized the character in which they are contained.

But if phonetics don't always carry true phonetic information, and signific elements are not always very significant, the characters of this class can still offer extremely useful tools to the talented poet. Detached from their codified dictionary meanings, the elements within a character may function independently, answering to the needs of the creative artist's imagination. For example, the suffix meaning "before" or "in front of" in Chinese includes among other elements a pictographic representations of a moon. The elements are there in the character originally to help to give a guide to pronunciation. But a poet who wants to talk about the pain of separation, while gazing upon the moon, like Li Po in "Thoughts of a Quiet Night," the famous poem found here on p. 90, can introduce an extra moon into a line by simply using what comes out in English translation as the appropriate preposition. Li Po's famous line "Before the bed, bright moonlight" actually contains among its five characters a moon (the pictograph for moon) and two more moons, one in the compound ideograph *bright* and another shining dimly but insistently out of the character for the preposition *before*. The moon, which can be seen at the same time in different places by separated friends, lovers, or family, is a powerful ready-made symbol. The writing system lets Li Po literally fill his little poem with moonlight.

Contemporary Chinese readers pay little or no attention to such possible manipulations of the language when they are reading a history, a scientific paper, or the daily news (though modern print advertisers *do* use these three-thousand-year-old "artifacts" in some pretty nearly subliminal advertising techniques). Moreover, not many traditional Chinese poems contain any character "tricks" of any kind. *Meaning*, the content of the poet's heart and mind and the message that heart and mind wishes to send another human, is almost always the purpose of the poem, at least of any poem I would translate. But the tools of the writing system are nonetheless clearly there. The best poets use them most, and put them to use best; sometimes, I'm sure, they play this way simply to show that they can, and sometimes, as in Li Po's "Thoughts of a Quiet Night," they do it seemingly effortlessly, as if the poetry gods had provided them with antic strokes in honor of a noble effort.

When, at last, I begin the run through of poets included in this book, I'll begin with an anonymous peasant, or peasants, who cared little for "form."

But before I present them, one more little technical bit: poets write in forms, such as sonnets or heroic couplets or free verse, and it's customary in any kind of poetry anthology to talk a little about the forms presented. This anthology contains poems in nine different forms. Two of them developed during the late Chou, in the fourth century B.C.E., outside the Chinese cultural realm in the state of Ch'u, and though the examples from these styles are important poems, the *form* did not continue as a vehicle for literary creation after the very early Han, two hundred years later.

Five of the most important forms are very closely related and can be seen as having evolved from the simple verses found in the *Poetry Classic*, or *Shih Ching*. All five of the forms share end rhyming on even numbered lines, with a rhyme on the first line optional. For all of the forms except the four-character verse found in the *Shih Ching*, both five- and seven-character lines are permitted, with a pause, or caesura, immediately before the final three characters in the line. Four of the five can be written to any length (any number of lines), if we don't quibble about a subdivision that observes an eight-line limit, and another that allows only four lines.

Each of these forms is a kind of *shih*. The word *shih* can refer either to one of these forms or to poetry in the generic sense.

Of the seven forms that survived the Han or were invented after it, the eight-line *lu-shih*, or "regulated *shih*," was technically the most demanding, being the only form in general use that forced the poet to take into account the fact that tone, the change of pitch over the course of a syllable, was a feature of the Chinese language. Interestingly, the strict rules of the *lu-shih* made it easy to write good verse — that is, to learn and to follow rules — and hard to write real poetry — to follow all the rules and still express clearly and fully what weighs on your heart and mind. Most poets of T'ang and after, even the wild Li Po himself, wrote *lu-shih*, peer pressure making them feel compelled to prove they *could*, perhaps. Tu Fu's reputation as China's greatest *human* poet, second only to Li Po, who was regarded as the spirit of poetry incarnate, rests partly upon his absolute mastery of the *lu-shih*.

The last two of the original forms mentioned above, the *tz'u*, practiced most seriously by Sung poets, and the *san-ch'u*, the short lyric variety of *ch'u* most popular among the unemployed bohemian-style poets and popular dramatists of the Yuan, were not widely pursued vehicles for serious poetry after the periods of their origination. Each of these forms involves "filling in" the metrical demands of, that is, putting words into, a preexisting song, as if you, or Weird Al Yankovich, were to write new words to "Yankee Doodle" or "The Star-Spangled Banner" or "Feelings." Many very fine poems, including the complete works of Li Ch'ing-chao, were written in the *tz'u* form, but the addition of tonal rules, à la the rules of the T'ang *lu-shih*, effectively stifled whatever freedom the folk origin of these forms brought with them. By the time of the Ming and Ch'ing, *tz'u* and the several kinds of *ch'u* writing became more or less a poetaster's hobby.

Now, though, we are ready to talk poetry and poets, and you may trust no poetaster is to be found anywhere ahead.

Anonymous is without a doubt the most prolific poet in the world. And I'm convinced that more often than not in world literature, Anonymous is a woman's name. Certainly, anyway, that's most often the case in this book. Rough-voiced as it is, "The Peasant's Song" might or might not be an exception to my rule. At any rate, this poem is identified by Mencius and Chuang Tzu, respectively two of the most important of the founding fathers of Confucianism and Taoism, as the first poem ever uttered in Chinese. Its radical, even anarchical ("What has some emperor to do with us?"), vision of local autonomy may be surprising to some readers. But perhaps we are just still influenced by old stereotypes regarding traditional Chinese ideas about personal freedom and "human rights." The poem's theme is certainly an honorable expression of the ideals of democracy as well as a perennial feminist one. It's also one that you'll find again and again in the poetry of Li Po and his friends in both temporal directions.

Following "The Peasant's Song" is a group of poems from the *Shih Ching*, a book regarded as a bible by orthodox Confucians for the past 2,500 years. Let me emphasize here that every poet in this book, Confucian or otherwise (save perhaps *the peasant* if we accept the dating of Mencius and Chuang Tzu), knew by heart all the poems from the *Shih Ching*. Like the Christian Bible in the English poetic tradition, the sacred status of all of the Confucian Classics makes these poems, even the most rough and ready among them, ripe for use as powerful allusions in later poetry.

The first nonanonymous poem in the Chinese tradition, the famous "On Encountering Sorrow" (*Li Sao*) by Ch'u Yuan, and the Taoistic response to Ch'u Yuan seen in "The Fisherman's Song," finish the offerings from the pre-Han period. Their content is extraordinarily influential in later traditional poetry.

After a selection from the Han's extant poetry, the most important poets of the Chinese dark ages are presented, and the works of Juan Chi and T'ao Ch'ien, among a group of notables, certainly point to the universal verity of the Western saying that hard times make for great art. Juan Chi is ambiguous and philosophically deep, and he is a source for T'ao Ch'ien, perhaps China's first "modern" poet, and many after him.

The sheer number of poets whose outstanding poems fill part 3 makes it clear that the T'ang dynasty, from which all the poets and poems that fill those pages are drawn, is, as the Chinese themselves assert, the Golden Age of Chinese poetry. First among many giants of the period comes Wang Wei, who would in any other generation have been a man without peer. He was a child prodigy as a musician, the innovative founder of a Zen-influenced school of landscape painting, and an important patron of Zen itself. He was also a high minister of state and a poet who mastered the T'ang quatrain, a verse form perfectly fitted to his synthesizing intellect and his Zen-trained powers of perception.

Immediately following Wang Wei in our pages, and in fact born less than a year after him, comes the truly incomparable Li Po. Though a difference between the length of one foot in his time and today makes this legendary eight-footer measure in at something closer to a modern six feet eight, he was a literary giant by any measure. Born and raised in China's western borderlands, he studied the art of swordsmanship while he also mastered the civil arts of poetry and philosophy in a Taoist monastery during his youth. Perhaps the world's first cultural "superstar," he composed verses on the spot to please an emperor or to settle a bar bill.

Just a page or so away from Li Po is to be found his younger contemporary and friend and China's other claimant to the title of "greatest poet," Tu Fu, a devoted family man who was also a dangerously courageous civil servant in an empire under siege. A generation later, in the footsteps of these master poets comes another wave of greats, including "the poet's poet" Po Chu-i, perhaps the second best known and certainly for a long time the single most translated of all the Chinese poets. Swelling the ranks of his generation are a trio of extraordinary poets, including Tu Mu, a somewhat guiltily committed hedonist, who was a relative of Tu Fu (and a master of the quatrain to rival even Wang Wei and Li Po); the mad, macabre genius Li Ho; and the Casanova of Chinese poetry, Li Shang-yin.

Because of the special themes of their poems, I have separated six poets of the T'ang from their contemporaries and placed them in a section of their own at the end of part 3, out of order in the book's chronological arrangement. All six are known as Zen poets. They include both monks and laymen. Three are pseudonymous or perhaps even entirely legendary, two were historically important men in the history of Zen Buddhism as an institution, and one was an apostate monk who went on to a successful career as a local official in a time when the famous bodhisattva oath (to dedicate oneself to serve humanity with unlimited compassion, refusing to enter nirvana until all other sentient beings were saved) may indeed have called humane and compassionate mortals to service in the red dust of the profane world. Their talents and skills mark them as members of the same tradition as Juan Chi and T'ao Ch'ien; and though Zen holds them apart from the lay poets of T'ang, *wen* binds them to the tradition of the Chinese person of letters.

When we return to history from our side trip into the sacred space-time of Zen, we discover T'ang drawn to an end and the number of great poets about to grow markedly fewer. The Sung did produce great poets. It offers Su Shih (also known as Su Tung-p'o) as an arguable rival for the title of greatest of the great. And Li Ch'ing-chao, wife of a Sung official from whom she was tragically separated, is the unquestioned best of all of traditional China's women poets.

But, to speak frankly, from the thirteenth century to the present there are really only a few truly outstanding poets. Of course there is no simple reason for the decline: with the growth of printing came the rise of colloquial prose forms, theater, the short story, the novel, and these, as in our own time, were forms that became popular and commercially successful. Printing meant that a literatus could make a living from his (or, if sufficiently masked from public recognition, perhaps even her) literary talents alone, without service as an official or even without official patronage. In both the Yuan and the Ch'ing dynasties, poets who would in better times have traditionally put their talents at the service of the government might even have considered it patriotic to have taken their literary talents into theater or popular commercial prose fiction as a protest against alien rulers (the Mongols of Yuan, the Manchus of the Ch'ing). And, just perhaps, the poets of later dynasties suffered from the very weight of their tradition. Certainly most of the poets who did write in classical forms during the Ming and the Ch'ing dedicated themselves intentionally to the *imitation* of either the T'ang or the Sung masters rather than to the conscious pursuit of originality. When imitation was the name of the game in poetry, we can expect only a few defiantly original voices, and that is what we get.

Luckily for our anthology, we can choose from the poems of only those few. There are the funny drinking songs of the out-of-work poet-officials manqué of the Yuan, and the wonderful rant of the first great Chinese dramatist, Kuan Han-ch'ing, whose "Not Bowing to Old Age" is an urbanite's bit of antinomianism to match anything "The Peasant Song" has to offer. There is the wonderful set of twenty quatrains by the Ming Zen master Han-shan Te-ch'ing, rendered here, as are the poems of Li Ch'ing-chao and the extraordinary Hsu Wei of the Ming, by the brilliant translator James M. Cryer. And there is no doubt in my mind that only a few of even the T'ang greats are equals of Yuan Mei, the sometime official of the Manchu Ch'ing, a man who may have seen Europeans in the flesh and who, like Benjamin Franklin, sometimes read with "eye-glasses." Ching An, the hardworking and good-humored Zen abbot, and Su Man-shu, the fake monk, both subjects of the Ch'ing, are both also outstanding poets. It is interesting to note that a consistent feature of the originality of all these Ch'ing dynasty poets is their ability to fit colloquial language into the classical forms, and though both Yuan Mei and abbot Ching An deny that they imitate either T'ang or Sung masters, both write in the purely classical *shih* forms, ignoring both the *tz'u* popularized by the Sung poets and the *san-ch'u* lyrics begun in the Yuan. Both poets sought a contemporary audience, but both also clearly honored classical poetry by writing it.

So, I might say, go to it. But I have one more thing to say before I let you go (says the old professor, who's closing in on forty years of working at translating some of these poems): though language, technique, and form are always extremely important in helping the artist deliver his or her message, that message—content and not form—is the point of poetry. Li Po proves his worthiness not by a trick with the moon elements in "Thoughts of a Quiet Night," a quatrain that is nearly untranslatable. He proves it with the accomplishment of a will to communicate something important, something simple for children and old folks: "Home is where the heart is, don't go far afield." It is something very different for the deep reader, the man and woman of the world, the striver toward whatever goal. "Home is where the heart is, don't go far lightly afield: even art and imagination *may not* be able to lead you home again." In a final reading it may simply say to the older reader, "Go home," whatever that may mean. Perhaps it's a pale shadow of this poem that awaits you in translation on p. 90. In the original it is the world's best-known poem, even today. In traditional times illiterates could chant it by heart. In the 1980s I heard a recording by a Cantonese children's choir that sounded strangely familiar (my Cantonese was just barely usable), and when I looked up the words (the characters allowing me to read the lyrics in Mandarin, the only kind of modern spoken Chinese of which I had any command), I found the nursery lullaby constructed around the Li Po poem and a few la-la-la's in the choruses. Li Po became and has continued to become, across well over a thousand years and many "language barriers" of time and space, the grandpa, the loving godfather singing a lullaby, for millions of Chinese children. *Wen* has made a family of all these people, a family of people who may stay at home and live rich lives or travel abroad in the great world, with old Grandpa or new friend Li Po at their sides.

Welcome to the best of my life's work and a sample of my friend Jim Cryer's inspired translations. Perhaps you will be taking the first step that begins the journey to the worldwide village of the future where Li Po and his friends are dwelling. I hope so.

PART ONE

From Before: The Beginning

Poetry from the Beginning of the Zhou Dynasty
(1122 B.C.E.) to the End of the Han (220 C.E.)

Introduction to Poetry from the Beginning of the Zhou Dynasty to the End of the Han

BEFORE PEOPLE BEGAN TO HERD DOMESTICATED ANIMALS and till the earth, they painted, they put flowers on the graves of their loved and honored dead, and without any doubt, they sang, alone and together, speaking to their gods, wooing a mate, lamenting what is always lost in living, and celebrating the miracle of life itself. So the peasants of "The Peasant's Song" dug their wells, cultivated their fields, and sent a message in song to whomever claimed hegemony over their land and their lives. Perhaps the first song in this anthology was indeed written even before the "first," which is to say *mythical*, dynasty, the Hsia, in a time when the emperors were True Sages, ruling solely by the emanations of their personal virtues and passing on rule not to their own kin but to the most virtuous subject they could discover. Whether or not this poem is authentically "prehistoric," it seems to me, with its theme of individual freedom so central to all Chinese poetry and all Chinese life, a perfect place to start.

The *Shih Ching*, usually translated as either the *Book of Songs* or the *Poetry Classic*, is the first great collection of Chinese poetry. Tradition says that it was edited into its present form by the Sage of Sages, Confucius himself. In fact the book was assembled before, during, and after the life of Confucius. Its more than three hundred poems include fragments of works as old as the Shang dynasty (traditional dates, 1766–1154 B.C.E.) as well as "contemporary" poems from the Chou feudal states written or spoken by both aristocratic court figures and just plain folks. A great deal has been said about the origin of many if not the majority of the poems as oral "folk" art, but it is clear from the artistry of the written language in which they have been handed down that, like the scribes who improved upon the originally oral poetry attributed to Homer in the West to create the *Iliad* and the *Odyssey*, the people who converted Chou folk songs and court verses into poetry in written Chinese characters clearly thought of themselves as (*and were*) artists. So the characters used to render simple and direct lyrical utterances of the illiterate peasant folk often honor them with carefully chosen written vocabulary: the heart and soul of folk art remains clearly present, but literary subtleties, the polish and the decoration that are *wen*, are introduced. The scribes who created the *Shih Ching* were poets, not tape recorders. They chose the best of what existed, and they honored its soul with their own art.

In its present form, the *Shih Ching* consists of three major sections. The *Kuo Feng*, or "Odes of the States," comprising the first 160 of the 305 poems, are generally but not always folk songs. The *Ya* ("Elegant Verses"), subdivided with no obvious criteria into greater and lesser, include poems 161 through 265, and the *Sung*, or "Temple Odes," high ritual songs and bits of dynastic myth, include poems 266 through 305. Of the present selection, except for a single longer poem on drinking and its positive and negative consequences that is found among the "Lesser Elegants," all come from the *Kuo Feng*.

The form of almost all the verses in the *Shih Ching* is extremely simple. There are four characters in each line, almost always divided by a caesura. Rhymes occur on all even-numbered lines (the second, the fourth, and so on) and also anywhere else the poet feels like putting one. It is assumed that part of the reason for the simple and rather abrupt rhythmic nature of the *Shih Ching* poems is the fact that they were performed to the simple percussion music of bells and drums, the only music of which Confucius approved, except in the privacy of his home, where he enjoyed playing the "lute." The character for *shih* came to be the general name for poetry, but the four-character line was seldom used, usually only for high ritual or religious purposes, after the beginning of the Han dynasty (206 B.C.E.).

Knowledge of the *Shih Ching* poems was a necessity of diplomacy around the time of Confucius, when it was a common practice to deliver or at least support the delivery of diplomatic messages among the feudal domains (states, or *Guo* of the *Guo Feng*) by oral presentation of relevant lines from the *Poetry Classic*. From the Han onward, many of the poems were imbued with very specific allegorical interpretations, but it is clear that later poets, who memorized the book word for word, used it as allusive material in their own poems at least as often for its plain "folk" messages as for its orthodox allegorical meanings. The numbers that serve as titles of these poems in this anthology are their numbers in the traditional editions of the *Shih Ching*.

Confucius and the peasant singers of the *Shih Ching* were people of north China, where the Chou dynasty states had spread in the watershed of the Yellow River and its major tributaries. The next two poems in this section come from the warmer and more fertile Yangtze valley, from the south Chinese state of Ch'u, nominally subject to Chou but proud possessor of its own very different cultural traditions. Ch'u Yuan (343?–278 B.C.E.), author of one and subject of the other of these works, was China's first nonanonymous poet. An aristocrat, he served as a court official and diplomat during Ch'u's struggle with the powerful and warlike Chou state of Ch'in. Eventually, fifty years after Ch'u Yuan's disappearance from the scene, Ch'in won the struggle to topple Chou. It founded the short-lived but well- (and ill-) remembered Ch'in dynasty, the first true unified Chinese dynasty under the infamous Emperor Ch'in Shih Huang-ti.

Ch'u Yuan was a Ch'u loyalist, even a protonationalist, and his poetic work makes the case for the cultural superiority of his south Chinese homeland, with its luxuriant scenery and romantic shamanistic religion (complete with dancing priestesses who communicated directly with the gods), over the dry and severe Confucian civilization of Chou's dry and severe northern homeland. He took the forms of his new poetry from the songs of the shamanesses, who performed their ecstatic dances to the music of woodwinds. These Ch'u forms, the earliest called Song style in clear reference to the sacred songs of the dancers, and the later, called Sao style, after Ch'u Yuan's great poem *Li Sao* ("On Encountering Sorrow") that is its finest representative, are much more formally elaborate than the *shih* poems. They are clearly an outgrowth of the shamans' singing, and yet they are also something completely, amazingly new. Line length was nearly doubled from the *shih*, and a rule required the creation not only of complex sentences (which the *shih*'s short lines and "end stopping" made very difficult to achieve) but also of elaborate grammatical parallelism. It is an expansive form, a romantic one, and as you will find in the *Li Sao* itself, one that Ch'u Yuan used perfectly to achieve an epochal, earth-shaking work.

It was a major feat for the scholars and literati of the Han— which followed immediately upon the short-lived Ch'in, which had wiped out Ch'u as well as all the other statelets of the Chou— to "capture" (through learned commentary on his greatest poem) the arrogant aristocratic and romantic southerner for the service of Confucian virtue. Had they failed, his poetry might well have served as a rallying point for regional separatism in the various periods in Chinese history. In his masterwork *Li Sao* there is only one place where the word *Chou* is used to refer to the Chou dynasty. In all its other appearances it appears in combinations that have negative connotations.

Interestingly, while the *Li Sao* and other poems of Ch'u remained popular among the traditional audience into the twentieth century, both the Song and the Sao styles' *forms* completely disappeared from use.

The *Li Sao* is the longest major poem in Chinese and has therefore sometimes been called China's epic, but as you will see, it lacks several of the requirements (blood and gore, for starters) of a Western-style epic. It may not have been Confucian in its major thrust in Ch'u Yuan's eyes, but it is certainly a great work of *wen*. Confucius found all so-called southern music "lewd," and he might have had a quibble here and there with Ch'u Yuan's propensity to imaginative exaggeration, but *Li Sao* was written by a cultivated, civilized gentleman, one who valued loyalty and personal honor, and I suspect that the Master would at last perhaps grudgingly have approved.

The other poem from Ch'u culture that I have included, "The Fisherman's Song," is something else altogether. Interestingly, this poem is traditionally attributed to Ch'u Yuan. I suggest you try reading it from that point of view. More likely some naughty Taoist "forged" it. Certainly most of the poets of the past two thousand–plus years have taken it as mockery of Ch'u Yuan's philosophical position, if not of the poet himself.

The Chou fell gradually, to be ultimately superseded by the famous Ch'in dynasty, a veritable Reich that would last a thousand years but lasted no longer than Hitler's. It had no *wen* and left no literature, burning books instead. I offer two short poems from this period. One is attributed to Liu Pang, the peasant who became founder of the Han, and the other to the prince of Ch'u Hsiang Yu, who was his last rival for the throne. They are written in song forms closer to the Ch'u style than to the traditional *shih*. Hsiang Yu's is tragically romantic. Liu Pang's is a surprisingly Confucian utterance.

The final group of poems in this section, sometimes called the Nineteen Old Poems of the Han, sometimes just the Nineteen Ancient Poems, was assembled toward the end of the Latter Han dynasty (25–220), but their authorship is uncertain. Formally they are new, and the Han poets' invention is one that was to last two thousand years. According to a perhaps nearly historical legend, the discovery of the new forms began with governmental researches among the common people, in a government effort to "tap the lines" of campfire and marketplace folk songs for signs of incipient insurgency. The five- and seven–character-line poems (always with a caesura before the final three-character phrase) were, in a nice subversion of the government's plans, quickly adopted by the socially conscious Confucian state officers of Han as a means for, at first, covert antigovernment or at least pro-reform propaganda poetry . . . poems of political criticism anonymously circulated as if they were "leaks" from the Yueh-fu, the misleadingly named Music Bureau charged with collecting internal intelligence.

At the worst, this is an interesting legend. At any rate, with both its existing formal springs of poetry running dry, about to be left without a single form for their poetry, it is clear that Han poets went to *the common people*, beginning a historical practice of periodic creative rejuvenation from outside the elite. Maybe something like that is in the process of rejuvenating, or repopularizing, American poetry.

By the early years of the common era, poems in this form, ever after known as *yueh-fu* (and later as old-style verse as well), had begun their two-thousand-year journey into the twentieth century. Some of these poems are apparently in women's voices, and, though it was later a common practice for male poets to assume a feminine persona, readers should form their own opinions. Pan Chiao, the sister of the first state officer to openly write in this form, was herself a major intellectual figure of the Han, among the most famous scholars and authors of her time.

A mountain of scholarship has grown up around the "Nineteen Old Poems of the Han." A few of them deserve great fame, and most have become sources of allusion in the work of the "greats" and not-so-great poets who followed them. Certainly not nearly all of the nineteen poems support the theory of their origin among the common people. Carpe diem themes and pure aristo-cratic hedonism find plenty of place. Several of the most signifi-cant of the lines and phrases that serve as allusions for other poets are pointed out in the notes. I hope you will find pleasure when you run into words later on that you first found here.

The Peasant's Song

Sunups, we get to work;
sundowns, we get our rest.
Dig wells and drink,
plow fields, to eat:
what has some "emperor"
to do with us?

From the Shih Ching
♦ 1

Hid, hid, the mated osprey, she and he,
on the island in the stream.
Hid, like an omen, in seclusion that mild maiden.
Fit mate for our lord.
(How he *does* love
the hunting of them.)

Long or short, the water herb,
left, right, flows by.
Hid, like an omen, hid away that gentle girl.
Awake? Asleep he hunts,
hunts but taketh naught.
Awake, asleep his heart afield, embracing her.
The distance weighing on his heart (alas, a lass!).
Rolling so, and rolling back, he turns again, lies splayed agley.

The long, the short, of water's herbs;
as they flow by, we'll harvest.
Hid, thy future, Lord, that gentle girl
in duet of strings, her zither with thy lute, engage her.

The long and short of it:
from what flows: grasp the best . . .
Left and right, we pick and choose, the finest.
Hidden well, the virtuous maiden,
with the bells and drums of marriage Rites, befriend her.

◆ 16

This sweet pear, this great shady tree,
don't you dare prune it, much less cut at it!
The good Lord Shao found friendly shade beneath it once.

This sweet pear, this great shady tree,
don't you dare clip it, much less do damage to it!
The good Lord Shao spoke true beneath it often.

This sweet pear, this great shady tree,
don't you dare clip, don't bend a twig of it . . .
Here the good Lord Shao gave honest judgment, always.

◆ 17

Might I have walked the dewy paths with thee,
just before the dawning of the day?
Say it was a drenching dew indeed . . .

Who would say the bird has no beak,
when it has bored its way into my chamber.

Who would say your clan's not powerful,
that has brought me before this judge?

But though you have dragged me before this judge,
I swear that you shall not marry me!

Who would say that rat has no teeth,
when clearly it hath breached my wall.

Who would say your clan's not powerful,
that has brought me before this judge?
But though you have dragged me before this judge,
I swear I shall never follow you!

◆ 20
Ripe and Ready

Ripe and ready, our plums are.
There are still a lucky seven!
The gentleman who comes seeking now
will surely find the time auspicious.

Ripe! Already dropping! Only three remain.
A gentleman who seeks me
might well come now . . .

Ripe and ready; plums fall. We lay them in a basket.
Any gentleman who seeks me, let him speak up right now!

◆ 23
In the Wilds, a Dead Doe

In the wilds, a dead doe,
white rushes wrap it.

In spring's embrace, a girl,
and lucky the lordling
that treasured her there.

A stand of oaks, in the wilds,
a dead doe, in white rushes wrapped,
a girl, pure as jade.

"Oh, easy, undress, undress me, oh!
I care naught for my robe, my dear:
but can you keep the dogs from barking!"

◆ 26
Cypress Skiff

Afloat in this skiff of cypress wood,
afloat upon the flow . . .
Aflame, aflame, I cannot sleep,
and yet my grief's my secret,
and I'm not without the wine
to make bold sport of this journey!

My heart's no mirror:
you would not find your face there.
Oh, and I do have strong brothers,
undependable,
I have taken my case before them,
and met only with their anger.

My heart is not a stone,
will not be rolled about, nor toyed with.
My heart's no doormat;

won't be rolled up and put away.
I am a *woman*, righteous, upright

as the hearty mountain plum.
There *is* no fault, no flaw *in me*.
My grieving heart pales with the moon,
yet hates all pettiness . . .
The petty folk who throng my door,
and all their petty insults.

Silenced, my words, in a brooding heart . . .
Yet every day, awakening, the pettiness anew.

Suns for but a day dwell, moons move . . .
Let *them* give way, since they *will* . . .
I'll wear my sorrowing heart,
the same unlaundered robe, each day.

I'm silenced here, but let words fly,
where body never may, to fray.

◆ 31
Drumbeats

Drums beat, the rumble.
How we jumped at it, to ride off to War.
We dug in at the capital, threw up a wall around Ts'ao!
Now I turn homeward, alone.

Following Sun Tzu-chung,
we *pacified* Ch'en and Sung,

and then he wouldn't lead us home,
and our hearts failed us, and failed him.

Stay, and be stuck there?
We stayed long enough to lose all the horses,
and there we went after them
in among the trees
where the enemy lay in ambush.

An *Oath to the Death* is hard broken,
but we'd *done* what we'd *sworn* to do,
and we had made oaths, also, to our wives
to grow old together, hand in hand.

Alas, for those oaths of ours,
yet we feared not for our lives.
We wept at the distance,
by false lord made twice oath-breakers.

◆ 42
Quiet Girl

For the quiet girl, pretty little one,
I've waited at the corner
of the tall city wall.
Love her. Never get to see her.
Scratch my head, I; and shuffle feet.

Quiet girl! She's a temptress!
Gave me this red flute,
a flute red as flame.
My heart's word's, joy, is my fortune,
just to see such a pretty girl.

I'd lead her home: soft grass in a pleasant meadow:
weep there to see
a beauty so rare!
Or, may be, she is no beauty . . .
But some beauty gave me this!

• 43
New Tower

New Tower's a sheen,
but the Ho's flow is muddy,
and the fit mate she sought's
proved a toad, all unclean.

New Tower's scrubbed,
while the River flows fetid,
but the fine mate she searched for's
a low loathsome toad.

The fishnets we spread
sometimes take a goose.
Once hunted our lady a fair mate, oh yes.
And took her a pitiful hunchback.

• 44
You Took Ship

You took ship: floating, floating, noonday sun.
I'll swear my heart dwelt upon you,
in my heart you dwell secure.

You took ship: floating, floating, away.
I'll swear my heart dwells with you:
go freely, stay safe.

◆ 61
The River Is Wide

Who says the river's wide?
A reed'll ferry it.
Who says the state of Sung is far . . .
Tiptoe I see it!

Who says the river's wide?
There's just enough for a knife blade.
Who says that Sung is far?
I could be there this morning.

◆ 67
My Lord Is Full of Yang

My Lord and Master's full of *yang!*
Left hand on his organ,
right hand he calls me to his room.
His joy's that organ!

My Lord and Master's easy, pleased . . .
Left hand fanning,
right hand he beckons me come play.
His joy is certainly that organ!

◆ 100
Before the East Was Bright

I'm up before the east is bright . . .
Inside out and upside down,
with all my clothes on wrong way 'round!
All because the duke's court calls.

Before the sun's begun to chase the dew . . .
Inside out and upside down,
everything the wrong ways 'round,
it's orders! From the duke!

Break off a few willows to fence in a courtyard,
and all the mad fellows stand wide-eyed!
Some can't tell morning from midnight,
so I'm either too early, or late, outright.

◆ 133
No Clothes

Who claims he is ill clothed
shall share this very robe o' mine . . .
The king be raising an *army*, boys.
I'll share my lance and spear,
and we will strive together 'gainst his foe!

Who cries "ill robed"
shall share the very cloth lies next my skin.
The king be raising an *army*, boys!
I'll share my spear and shield;
we'll act as one.

Who'll still say that he's ill-clothed?
We'll wear the king's livery together.
The king be raising an army now.
I'll share my armor;
and we'll to war.

Willows of the East Gate

Eastgate's willows . . .
leaves full of dawn light.
Evening it was we set to meet; now,
morning star is blazing bright.

Eastgate's willow
leaves are emptied of the moonlight,
evening was our rendezvous.
Now morning star: and cutting shafts of sunlight.

Burying Ground

The burying ground is grown up, untended,
needs the axe now.
Our lord's not a good man,
and the whole country knows it.

Burying ground is plunged in wild
plum trees, that attract aught but owls,
birds of ill omen.

He's a bad man, and we all sing
songs to spread the word,
spread the word widely,
and yet he ignores it.
When he looks back on
his own undoing,
he will remember us then.

◆ 165
Felling Trees

Felling trees, the axes ring,
just so, a bird sings,
when she's flown from
a dark valley, into a tall tree . . .
Singing. Singing voice ringing,
to find out her flock.

Shall I not also sing,
with a song to find *my* fellows?
Even the spirits will hear it
and make harmony.

Felling trees the axes clack,
as I strain strong beer for festive giving,
and there's a fatted lamb
to feast my father's brothers.
Sure, and they may not come,
but none will fault *me* as unready.
Courtyard I've swept and sprinkled,
and laid have I the table with the eight grains,
companions to the lamb:

thus do I invite my mother's brothers.
And, sure, they may not come,
but none will fault me as unready.

They are felling trees upon the hillside
as I strain my good strong beer.
Dishes on the groaning board arranged,
and all my kin are here!
Many a great family has fallen awry
for a thing so small as a piece of the pie!
So while there be, I shall serve it myself,
and when there be none I'll go buy!
It's I myself shall be a-bangin' the drum,
and I myself shall be dancing . . .
and if I am ever to leave this work be . . .
Let it be only to toast each of thee!

◆ 220

The guests begin the feast
ranged about in perfect order:
with rare tidbits and overflowing bowls
laid out upon the festive board.
The wine is mellow. Drinking's
sure to bring us harmony.
With bells and drums accompaniment,
the loving cup's passed 'round.
Let men of great renown compete with pride,
with bows and arrows their ritual means.
The archers, matched in pairs,
dedicate their marksmanship to our liege lord.
"Shoot and find the mark:
another cup be thy reward."

Then dance to the flute and drum:
music of our harmony we offer up:
offer up to the shining ancestors,
performing here punctiliously
each and every facet of the rite.
And when all rituals have been carried through,
grandly and to fullness,
the ancestors bestow that greatest blessing:
sons and grandsons to follow us.
These joys call for music,
and all respond in chorus.
The loving cup goes from hand to hand
again among the guests,
and the house men all join in again.
Oh, let the cup now be filled once more,
let's see what they can make in concert!

When the guests begin the feast,
gentle men they are, and reverent.
And *before* they get *drunk*,
they're upright and proper, true to their places.
Oh, but say they *do* get drunk . . .
"upright and proper" become "stumble and scramble"
as leaving their places they trip, dance, and ramble.
When they're not yet *too* drunk, they're upright and proper . . .
When I say they're "drunk"?
They don't know their places.

When they're drunk, they hoot and they howl,
kick over the tables and prance all around.
When people are drunk, they don't know the boundaries,
with their hats on crosswise,
they resort to lewd dancing.

If they leave when they're drunk,
they are blessed as the rest are.
If they get drunk and stay,
the feast's power's weakened.
To drink wine is good omened,
when it's done with restraint.

Thus be it ever with the drinkers of wine:
some will get drunk and some will stay sober.
So we stand up a censor,
and appoint a recorder.
Since the drunks all do wrong,
and offend those in order,
we will stop them from speaking
or acting awry.
What may not be spoken of is best left unspoken,
what comes forth from meanness is best left unsaid.
What comes forth from drunkenness
is like horns on a lamb.

If you can't handle the spirits
of the three ritual cups,
how *dare* you take more.

Ch'u Yuan (343?–278 B.C.E.)

Li Sao (*On Encountering Sorrow*)

Scion of our great ancestor Kao-yang,
Po-yung was my father's name.
When the stars of the She-t'i constellation

dwelt in the house of the first moon,
on the *keng-yin* day, I was born.
My father, seeing the signs and portents of my birth,
divined, and chose for me appellations of the purest fortune.
For my own name he gave me Upright Exemplar;
for my formal title, Spiritual Balance.
Inborn beauty was mine from the start;
I cultivated my talents and adorned my spirit,
picking river sage and fine angelica to wear,
and twisting autumn orchids in my belt.
In my cultivation I raced on, as if in fear of never catching up,
as if anxious that the years would not deign to take me with them.
Mornings I gathered magnolias on the mountainsides,
evenings I gathered winter grasses upon the riverbank.
Days and months fled me, never slackening their pace,
springs gave way to autumns, their dynasties in train.
Watching the leaves and grasses wither and drop,
my heart came to fear my Fair One's own slow certain sunset.
Unable to resist maturity, abhorring the harvest,
yet might I not abate this passage?
I'll harness the finest team, and drive abroad!
Come, find *my* Way, I will be there to lead.

So pure was the virtue of the Three Ancient Lords
that all that was fragrant was with them:
The pepper of Shan mixed with dwarf cinnamon;
there was more than just valerian and angelica.

And Yao and Shun? Bright-burning, determined,
they honored the Tao and found the straight road.
But Chou and Chieh, stampeding, ran wild,
sought shortcuts and strode into *pits* with imperious strides,
stealing their pleasures by dark shadowed roads ranged with perils.

Though I never trembled for fear of such as these,
I dreaded to see my lord's carriage go by ways such as those.
So I ran ahead and searched behind,
seeking the tracks of the Former Kings.
But my Lord failed to see my inner feelings,
and turned on me in rage.
My honest counsels brought me only troubles, surely,
but I endured, could not desist.
May the Ninth Heaven bear witness to my righteousness:
all that I did I did for Him.

At first He spoke to me with honest words,
but then, regretting it, He turned his glance on other ways.
I am one who can bear up against a parting,
but I sorrowed that my Lordly One should be inconstant.

Oh! Once I had planted full nine fields of orchids,
and a hundred acres of valerian,
I cultivated peonies, and cart-halt's bloom,
wild ginger, and sweet angelica.
And all these fields where my hopes were sown
grew both luxuriant and tall.
The cutting at harvest's in no way a harm:
but I grieved as they grew up in weeds.

The mass of men thrust forward, lusting.
Who could trust these?
Dogs at their meat, wanting more:
goatish, obstinate, and trusting all men their equals,
each avid with envy and hatred for all.

Do I rush forward to follow?
Such things are not what sets my heart racing:

old age comes in slow step, but it comes,
and I fear I've left no name to stand beyond me.

In the dawn I sip magnolia's dew,
at dusk I sup the fallen petals of chrysanthemum.
My faith is true beauty, and I am steadfast.
What matter if my face grow lean and sallow.

I weave a twine of woody rootlets, fair angelica,
and string it with the fallen stamens of the cassia,

plait cinnamon with heliotrope,
to make long lithe loops with creeper.

I make my pattern the way of worthy men of old
and will not wear the clothes of this world's vulgar men,
I shall not follow where the leaders of this day may lead,
I depend upon and may well end upon old P'eng Hsien's model.

Long I sigh deep to hide my tears,
grieving that the people's lives are made so hard.
Though I offer up the old ways to my Lord,
I'm bound up in pretty slanders, in the morning
a counselor; in the evening, in exile.

In exile I may yet wear a sash of heliotrope,
and gather still more angelica.

This is what my heart and mind are good for,
and if I died nine deaths for these, I could not grieve.

I despised my Sainted Lord's vast fecklessness,
who never sacrificed to learn his people's hearts.

And yet his many women envied me my beauty,
and whispered all my skills were bent on grasping *him*.

For they and all the vulgar of these times are *crafty*,
grasping the ruler and square to straighten things *wrongly*
mocking the chalk line and drawing things *crooked*
making the ways of wicked Chou their only measure.

All bound about, I feel frustrated and uncertain:
Am I the only one who feels the hardship at living in these times?
I'd rather die a wandering exile
than stand here witnessing to these.

Eagles do not fly in flocks;
so has it ever been.
There is no squaring circles;
those on different ways go different places.

Yet to humble the spirit and curb the will,
to stand up to calumnies, and endure slanderous tongues,
to stay pure and clean, to die standing straight:
these things the Ancient Sages all extolled.
Yet in my heart I knew I too had failed
to aid my Lord divining the true path,
and I tarried, about to turn back,
then wheeled my chariot onto the old road anew,
before I'd gone so far as to lose my way.

I walked my horses by the orchids on the marsh banks,
then drove them on to rest beneath the hillside pepper trees.
I would advance no further forward into blame,
rather retreat and search out my old raiment:
I plaited a robe with chestnut and lotus,

and gathered hibiscus blossoms for the skirt.
None truly knows me . . . so may it be,
so long as my heart's good faith remain fragrant.

Let my hat be a tower, a peak, and my sash so long it trails me,
though I may appear a tattered tangle beneath the perfume,
in the bright matter of my being, there's yet no flaw.

So, suddenly I turned about, to let my eyes wander:
I would go to visit the four quarters of the world.
My belt still flowered with adornments,
their fragrance floating far.

Every person's born with predilections.
Am I alone in loving beauty, and its truth eternal?
Let me be carved by the butcher, I'll never change . . .
No such fate as that makes my heart tremble.

Then my sister Nu Hsu cried in a quavering voice,
again and again beseeching me in warning,
"Gun, too, was so stubborn,
with no thought of his own being
and fighting the Great Flood, he perished on the plain.
Why must you be haughty, addicted to beauty?
Why must you alone adorn yourself so?
Thorns and weeds fill up the Lord's court;
why set yourself apart, refusing to dress yourself so?
You can't speak face to face with all of the people.
None will be moved if you say 'look deep into my heart.'
Today men rise by forming cliques,
why must you stand alone, not listening even to me?"

"I depend upon the Ancient Sages to keep me chaste:
I depend upon my heart to carry me through this.

I'll cross the Yuan and the Hsiang, heading south.
I'll plead my case before Ch'ong Hua."

Ch'i's Nine Dances and Nine Songs,
brought down from Heaven:
The Lords of Hsia loved these alone,
and so let themselves wander,
with no thought to a backward glance,
and none to looking forward . . .
and the five sons made play with arrows even in the family halls.
Yi was a wastrel wanderer, the arrows of the hunt his only thought;
how he loved to bend his bow against the wily fox!
But random rushing rushes toward foul ends,
and his own house man Han Cho stole his lady.
Cho's son Chiao, dressed in stout armor,
went where lusts led him, all unrestrained,
his days lost to pleasures, until he was lost,
and *his* head came tumbling down.
Chieh of the Hsia made wrongs his right,
followed *that* way, and found disaster.
Lord Hsin pickled and salted his ministers of state,
and such a state as that Yin of his did not outlast him.

T'ang, Yin's founder, and Yu, the father of all Hsia:
these two were solemn and respectful,
and the men of the Chou kept carefully to the Way.
Raising up upright men, using the skillful,
staying to the chalk line of the carpenter's cord.
The Way of Heaven knows no favorites,
judging and aiding men in proportion to their virtue.
Only the Sage finds success in action
and is fit to rule here down below.
I have gazed upon causes, upon consequences,

and watched the plans of peoples to their ends.
And who have I found of use but the righteous,
who shall serve but the good?
I have come to stand on the cliff of danger,
yet when I look how I came here
I do not know regret.
Bringing a straight handle for a faulty tool . . .
Many a worthy man of old died for this "crime."
Anxious and gloomy I've sighed,
moaned that my times are so out of joint.
I plucked soft lotus petals to wipe away my tears,
and yet they wet my collar, wave on wave,
as I knelt in my robes and gave vent to these words,
that my upright heart be heard.

Then I yoked four dragons of jade to the phoenix chariot,
and on a rising wind I rose.
In the dawn I set out toward Ts'ang-wu,
by eventide I'd reached the Hanging Gardens.
I'd hope to rest by its sacred gates,
but the sun of a sudden sank and set.
I ordered the sun's charioteer, Hsi Ho, to desist,
and to linger above mountainous Yen-tzu a while.
It's a slow road I go
as I search high and low.

I watered my horses at the pool of Hsien
and tied the reins to the Fu-sang tree,
breaking a branch from the very tree,
to make me a quirt to slow the sun down.

Then I sent Wang Shu to scout ahead,
Pure Breeze, the moon's charioteer, to lead my rearguard,

and the Sky-Emperor Bird to herald my coming.
But the Thunder God reported that all was not yet ready.

So I ordered my phoenix-steeds to rise and fly,
on and on through days and nights.
Whirlwinds rose up to greet me,
leading clouds and rainbows out to meet me:
a fluttering confusion of partings and joinings,
high and low their brilliant colors on display.

But when I ordered Heaven's gateman to open for me,
he lounged on the gate and gazed right past me.
The day at dusk, sky darkening,
I fingered my orchid sash, and stood in indecision.
This world is mud: I can't get clear.
Whatsoever be pure is jealously hidden.

When morning came I forded the White Water,
climbed Lang-feng's peak to tether my horses there.
Heart flagging, I gazed about, and wept:
there was no Fair Lady there.
Yet having arisen to this Temple of Spring,
I snapped off a branch of jasper there to add to my belt,
and before the glorious flower was faded,
I'd seek out some maiden below, to whom I might offer it.

Then I ordered Feng Lung to mount on the clouds,
and seek out lady Fu-fei's dwelling.
I untied my sash as a pledge of my troth,
and sent the Lame Beauty to be my go-between.

A flutter of confusion of partings and joinings
as, willful and obstinate, she made the way hard.

Evenings she'd be off again to Ch'ing-shih Mountain,
mornings wash her hair in Wei-p'an Stream.

She guarded her beauty in arrogance,
yet every day knew wanton play.
Though she's a true beauty, she follows no *rites* . . .
Come, leave her be, and seek elsewhere.
And elsewhere I looked, to the four ends of the earth,
twisting, like a stream through the heavens,
and then, coming down,
I gazed at the Jade Terrace on high,
and saw there the Lord of Sung's daughter.
I sent the Poison-Pinion Bird to make the match,
but he returned to say, "She's no fit mate."
Then yet again I sent him back . . .
and still I rue I ever used that chattering tongue.
My heart was vexed, my mind uncertain;
I should have gone myself, but that the rites forbade.
The Phoenix had offered the matchmaking gift,
and I feared Kao Hsin had gone before me.
Then I wished myself to some solitary perch
but there was no fit place to go,
and I, distracted, simply wandered on.
If Shao K'ang had not wed them,
I'd have stayed with Yu's daughters,
but those I'd sent to make my case were weak,
my go-betweens were crude and vulgar,
and I feared their words could never make a match secure.

The world is mud and muck, meets any worth with envy,
hating beauty, but praising every ugly thing.
Deep within the palace, hidden there, sequestered,
the wise king is threatened and yet will not awaken.

I must clasp close my feelings, and utter not even "alas!"
Can I go on like this forever?

I gathered bindweed and bamboo slips to make augury,
and asked Ling Feng to speak their omens.
"Two beauties will find harmony," said she,
"Who is truly beautiful and yet unloved?
You ponder the vastness of our Nine Provinces,
yet how can they be the only lands where ladies dwell?
Go forward far, all doubts aside.
There you may meet a beauty seeking yours.
Where is there a land with no fragrant herbs?
Why must you cling to this world that you know?"

My generation's subtle, hiding its ways.
Who among these may judge me, fair or foul.
Among the common folk good and bad are clear,
only the ruling clique is unable to distinguish . . .
They stuff their belts with smelly mugwort,
and say the orchid is not fit to wear.
Can't tell a blossom from a noxious weed,
how could they serve as judge of gems?
They cram their scent bags with manure,
and then say pepper has no fragrance.

I wanted to follow Ling Feng's lucky omens,
but my heart faltered and I doubted still.
Since the shaman Hsien was descending with the sun,
I spent of my own treasured store of pepper
to make offerings ready for her.
A hundred spirit creatures were arrayed awaiting.
Many-Doubts Mountain rose in welcome too.
A blinding white, the light of this spirit
proclaimed auspicious omens to me, saying,

"You must climb up high, and clamber down the deeps,
seeking after one of your own measure.
T'ang and Yu struggled to find fit companions,
and found Yi Yin and Kao Yao to be their ministers.
If your desire is pure and noble,
what need have you of a matchmaker?
Fu Yueh was building walls at Fu-yen
till Wu Ting gave him office and trust.
Lu Wang wielded but a butcher's blade,
yet when King Wen saw him he raised him high.
Ning Ch'i, as he toiled, sang out his heart's complaints
and Duke Huan of Ch'i found for him his fated place.
It's not late yet!
Your season's hardly come.
Don't fear the nighthawk's jarring cry might come early,
to strike down the hundred herbs before they can bloom."

And how splendid *is* the sparkle of my jasper belt.
In jealousy the crowd would keep it hid.
It is only this clique that can't be trusted.
These would plot to smash it, sure.

The times are out of joint, are shifty, changing.
Why should I linger here?
Even orchid and iris have lost their fragrance,
sweet flag and heliotrope, transformed to sedge.
How, and why, have the blooms of other days
all turned to noxious weeds?
What other reason can there be,
than that *they* all *hate* both truth and beauty?

I'd thought I could depend on Orchid,
but there's nothing real behind that made-up face.

He's spurned beauty to run with the crowd.
Might I still find him place among the fragrant?
And Pepper is all flattery and grasping insolence,
filling *his* scent bag with rank dogwood berry.
They labor only to advance and find preferment.
Would I bow to the odor of these?
Yet this is the way my world will go . . .
and who could live here without changing?
If Orchid and Pepper are so,
so much the more for Cart-halt and River Sage.

Only this belt of mine is worth calling noble:
its fragrance wafting, it's hard to find fault in.
I'll spurn "beauty" and stay here with this,
this fragrance that lingers today.

Or, finally, I'll follow my fancy,
and wander on idly in search of a girl.
While I'm yet adorned with the fullness of manhood,
I'll go where I will, and look high and low.

Since Ling Fen had already graced me with good omens,
and set a lucky day for me to leave,
I broke branches of carnelian
and ground that jewel to flour to bake waybread for my journey.
"Make ready the chariot that's drawn by flying dragons,
the chariot built of ivory and jade.
How could I dwell with ones so
far from the ideals my heart holds?
I'll journey long and hard just so as to dwell far from those."

I wended the way that leads to the Kun-lun Mountains,
a way hard and far, full of twistings and turnings.

Our banner of clouds gave shade from the sun,
but the jangle of harness bells sang of my sorrow.
In the dawn I set forth from Heaven-ford,
in the dusk took my rest at the world's western edge.

Phoenixes flocked to me, bearing my flags,
soaring, wings wide, in awesome array.
There, in the north, I reached Flowing Sands,
and finding the Red Waters, moved easily on.
I summoned horned dragons to bridge her for me,
and the God of the West, to escort me.

Yet this road too was long and hard,
and I sent orders for a change of route,
sent my escort to the left flank, around Pu-chou Mountain
setting our rendezvous for the West Sea.
We mustered there, a thousand chariots.
Jade hub to hub, we moved on ahead.
My eight dragon steeds flew before us, undulating,
wrapped in banners of cloud, like wreathes, as they flew.

I tried to curb my vaulting will,
and to slow their wilting pace,
but my spirit soared outward
to a realm beyond distance.
I sang the Nine Songs
and danced the sacred Steps of Shao.
But as I rose to the precincts of Heaven,
I chanced to glance down, upon my old home.
My groom lost heart, my horse too knew it.
They strained to look back, and would not go on.

Reprise:
In this land there is no man that knows me.

Why then should I cling to this city?
Since there is none who will stand with me in making just rule,
I shall go where P'eng Hsien guards the Way.

The Fisherman's Song

In banishment Ch'u Yuan wandered
by riverbank and marsh's edge, singing as he went.
His face dejected, his form wasted,
the fisherman caught sight of him.

"Art thou not great Ch'u Yuan, Lord of the Three Wards?"
the fisherman asked. "What can have brought you to *this*?"

"All the world is muddied, I alone am pure," said Ch'u Yuan.
"All the world is drunk, and I alone am sober, so I'm sent in exile."

"The wise are not chained to the things of the world, but can
move with the world as it moves. If all the world be muddy,
why not join in stirring the mud and thrashing up the waves?
If all men are drunk, why not drink their dregs and swill their
        leavings?
Why let deep thoughts and high hopes leave you exiled?"

"I have heard it said," Ch'u Yuan replied,
"that he who has just washed his hair should brush his hat,
and he who has just bathed should shake out his clothes.
How could I lay down my spotless purity upon the filth of others?
I would prefer to throw myself into the river's deeps,
and be buried in the bowels of fish, than to hide
my shining light in the dark and dirt of this world . . ."

The fisherman, smiling faintly, put his paddle in the water, to
        make off,
and as he went he sang:

> When the waters of the Ts'ang-lang are clear
> I can wash my hat strings in them
> When the Ts'ang-lang waters are muddy,
> I wash my feet in them.

And then he was gone, to be heard not again.

Hsiang Yu (230–202 B.C.E.)

Song at Kai-hsia

The strength of my arm plucked mountains up. Oh,
did it set the world in my shade!

But the time wasn't right, ah . . .
Now not even bold Dapple can break away.

And if even my Dapple be trapped? Ah,
then there is no hope for any deed.

Oh you, my Lady Yu, ah!
What hope could there be for thee . . .

Liu Pang (256–195 B.C.E.)

Song of the Great Wind

Great wind risen, oh!
Clouds, flying, scatter!

My hands hold all within the seas,
as I come back to where I was born!

Where shall I find fierce warriors,
where?
To guard the many feudal realms as One!

From *The Nineteen Old Poems of the Han*
◆ 1

On and on, and on and on again,
from you, my Lord, my love, I'm parted in this life.
Gone our own ways, each ten thousand *li*, to a horizon.
Those ways were difficult, and long;
might we come face to face again? How should we know?

Hunnish horses lean into the harsh north wind there,
while birds of Vietnam nest upon these warm southern
        branches.

The day we went our separate ways: that day's long gone.
Now day by day my gown grows loose upon me.
Floating clouds hide the vain day's passing,
and the wanderer doesn't look back, will not return.

Heart and mind dwelling on you, oh my Lord, I grow old,
as the harvest moon signals that the year grows late.
And so my heart will say no more than this:
try hard to stay well.

◆ 2

Green, green: the riverbank grass
Crowded, crowding, willows within garden walls.
Overflowing is the lady in the tower,
bright, bright, before the window.
Beautiful, so beautiful, that face, adorned with rouge.
Delicate, embroidery, the slender hand that gestures
by the window's lattice, there for all to see.

She was a geisha once.
Now she's a wastrel's wife:
a rambling man, who left and wanders still.
Chaste bed is hard to keep; empty, alone.

◆ 4

Today, we'll feast,
a feast words won't describe.
Lutes echoing our harmony
new notes, a magical music.
Let our power be sung aloud,
that those who hear may know the Truth!
Hearts in unison, we share one wish,
though we may keep that wish unspoken.
A man is born to live so short a life,

dust in the wind, no more.
Why not whip your horse to prancing,
and race across the ford to *Power*.
There's no reason to take pride in poverty!
Forever living but to sigh out bitter pride.

◆ 6

I forded the River to pluck the hibiscus,
and in the orchid marsh the many fragrant grasses:
To whom shall I give what I have taken?
The one I think of is on a far-off way;
does he still turn to gaze on his old home?
On the long road the distance slowly grows,
the single heart we share is forced to dwell in two places:
naught but grief and worry as slowly we grow old.

◆ 7

Bright moonlight glistens white upon night sky.
The house cricket sings by the eastern wall.
The Jade Scales point toward the beginning of winter.
Ah, how the constellations cycle through the seasons.
White dew, the frost draws omens on wild grass,
the time arrives when suddenly again begin the *Changes*.
Autumn cicadas sing in the trees.
Dark swallows, where, where have they gone?
Once I had a friend I dwelt and studied with,
now he's spread his wings and risen high indeed,
forgetting how we walked once, hand in hand.
He's left me, like footprints, behind.

In the southern sky, some see a *Winnowing Fan*,
  in the north, *The Ladle*,
And an *Ox* who'll never be yoked to plow . . .
Truly if goodness be not firm as stone,
False-titled "friend," what value's that?

♦ 10

Afar, far off, the Herd Boy,
White, bright, the maiden by the River in the Sky.
Slender, brocade, the pale hand she plies,
with shushing and sliding of shuttle on loom.
The livelong days she's never done:
tears, tears are raindrops falling.
The River in the Sky is clear, and shallow,
yet how shall they ever cross, to meet again.
Brimming, overflowing, those broad waters,
as they gaze and gaze, unable to find words.

♦ 11

I wheel the chariot about: I've yoked these steeds to drive,
far, far, across the ford and out upon the Way.
I gaze about me on the wasteland,
where spring's wind moves all the grasses.
Among the things that my eye meets is nothing *ancient*.
Yet I myself will soon grow old.
To flourish, to wither, each owns the time.
To win yourself a *place*? It's only bitter
if you wait too long.
No man's made of metal, none of stone:

how then to live for ever?
You'll go, you'll follow, quickly as *Things Change*.
Fame, a glorious *name*, is all that can last.

◆ 13

I drive my chariot up toward the East Gate
and gaze far off to the grave mounds, northward.
The poplars sigh. The graveyard pine and cypress,
as they flourish there, make the broad way narrow.
There, beneath, the ancient dead lie,
dumb shades in the eternal sunset,
sunk in sleep beneath the Yellow Springs.
A thousand years? Forever they will not awaken.
Vast is the ebb and flow of yin and yang.
The years of one's fate are a morning's dew.
A human life's an overnight abiding . . .
The man of greatest age is not as old as metal or as stone.
The myriads of years, come and go:
nor saint nor sage can go with them.
In fasting and sackcloth some seek
Immortality;
many have found in long-life drugs dead ends.
Better? Down good wine,
and dress in fine soft silks.

◆ 14

Those who have gone are each day farther,
so let us living, love, draw close.
Go out the door and look,

and all you'll see is grave mounds.
Old mounds, shorn and plowed, are fields again,
and graveside pines and cypresses are hewn for burning.
Wind through the graveyard poplars?
The heart would deny it if it could,
sighing, sighing, sad enough to die.
My heart is in those fields, the fields of home.
All I want is to return: there is no Way.

◆ 17

Solstice, quintessence of the cold is come;
north wind so cruel, hearts tremble.
In grief you come to know how long a night can be,
and raise your gaze to ponder on the wheeling constellations.
On the fifteenth night the bright moon, full:
on the twentieth, its face is cleft.
A traveler from afar has come
and brought a missive meant for me:
"I'll forever think of you," it opened
and ended "long though we be parted."
I've kept that letter in my sleeve
three years, the words unfading.
That my heart, alone, should cling to such a little thing . . .
My only fear, that you don't know.

◆ 19

Bright moon, how it glistens, glistens,
shining through the curtains of my bed.
Heart vexed and grieving, I cannot sleep.

Clasping my robes I rise and wander, pacing, back and forth.
Though they say that travel has its joys,
none's so great as early turning homeward.
Out the door, I'm pacing anxiously:
with whom to share this heart's sad thoughts of home?
Head bowed, at last I must go back into my chamber.
Tears fall: chill where they wet my gown.

PART TWO

A Time of Trials

Poetry from the End of the Han (220 C.E.)
to the T'ang (618 C.E.)

Introduction to Poetry from the End of the Han to the T'ang

THE HAN FELL NOT SO MUCH WITH A BANG AS WITH A
clatter: first crumbling into "The Three Kingdoms" (whence a
folk novel *The Romance of the Three Kingdoms* that is *still* to be rec-
ommended, for both entertainment and education about early
China). Then it shattered into seven or so little dynasties . . . imag-
ine, each with its totally serious pomp and circumstance . . . in the
North, and, in the South, first into *sixteen* kingdoms, and then at
last a dynasty that managed to last over a hundred years. Then four
more little kingdoms, before, finally, a true unification, under the
Sui Dynasty, that lasted twenty-nine years: and then, at last, to
the T'ang. At every level people made what lives they could. At the
top some luxury remained, and among our poets we find that, like
St. Francis, people of good will suffered shame for their share of
that luxury. Four horsemen rode: war itself killed soldier and refugee
alike. There was famine and pestilence for those who waited at
home, and death, for multitudes from many causes. Often it must
have seemed a liberation. And through these times history pro-
ceeded: Buddhism, introduced to the upper levels of society only
in the final century of the Han, saw its holy texts translated, tem-
ples and monasteries established and growing, while the majority
of ordinary folks let the more magical forms of Buddhism join Tao-
ism as a source of religious solace, and the elite joined other forms
of Buddhism to their Confucianism and Taoism in an attempt to
create ways of living fully, honestly, completely even in such times.
This Age was not so long as the European Dark Ages, and maybe
even not so dark. It was nonetheless one to prove the universal ver-
ity of the Western saying that bad times make great art. There was
plenty of empty court poetry, but some of the best of traditional
Chinese poetry was written during this period as well.

The two anonymous poems that begin the Han-to-T'ang selections show two very different attitudes, both clearly alive among the Chinese of the period. "Fought South of the City Wall" is very much a warrior's poem. Although China's philosophies do indeed honor a pacifistic stance, neither Confucians nor Taoists advise accepting defeat. Thus China is not without her martial heroes and heroines. "Going This Path," on the other hand, does honor the pacifists' Way. The pun on Tao, Way, is present in the original of the latter poem.

Juan Chi (210–263) was the most important of the Taoist eccentrics known as the Seven Sages of the Bamboo Grove. His best friend, Hsi K'ang (223–262), also a fine poet, was a lutenist and the first writer on music theory and practice. He was executed for showing less than abject obeisance to his disreputable emperor. All of the Sages, including the prototypical "drunken master" Liu Ling, were political and social critics, hiding their very ethical outrage behind a veil of eccentric behavior. Hsi K'ang was simply less subtle than his fellow sages. Juan Chi's poems in this anthology are drawn from his eighty-two poem set, *Yung Huai Shih (Songs of My Heart's Ideals)*.

T'ao Ch'ien (365–427), originally named Yuan-ming (Bright and Clear), changed his personal name to Ch'ien ("sunken" or "hidden") in response to the fall of the Eastern Chin (or Tsin) dynasty, under which he had served in several official capacities. Complicating the issue was the fact that he had also served the general who was the eventual usurper of the Chin throne. Known traditionally as a nature-loving, quietistic Taoist, a hermit farmer who was a lover of little children and of large quantities of wine, the actual man was a complex and very *modern* one, a great poet whose ethical standards were as high as his artistic ones. He was influenced by the poetry of Juan Chi and by the works of the Taoist relativistic philosopher-sage and humorist Chuang Tzu to write poems that expressed his own strengths and weaknesses honestly, giving him a solid stance from which to criticize his times. After his death he was without a doubt the most quoted and alluded to of all traditional poets, for at least a thousand years.

Hsieh Ling-yun (385–433) was a member of an aristocratic family that survived the Han-to-T'ang dark ages almost unscathed. His poetry is characterized by careful word choice. Its characters and phrases are packed with meaning from the inside (etymologically) to the outside (allusions and textual reference). These meaning-packed lines sometimes show a whiff of aristocratic arrogance (the rich often have such bad manners!), but they betray a hint or two of wistful, even rueful, self-knowledge as well. On the basis of his literary work, he was a minor official poet, only to die in a court mutiny.

Pao Chao (414–466) did not suffer from the disadvantage of high birth. His poetry reveals deep moral courage and strength of character. A man who could speak honestly about himself without shame, and share pain without instilling melancholy, Pao Chao was widely quoted in the T'ang, and afterward his reputation continued to grow.

Lady Tzu-ye (5th century?) is a name attached to a set of poems that are clearly anonymous folk songs. Their subject matter, though occasionally masked in euphemisms, is sexual love, and they mark the first time since the *Shih Ching* that this important facet of human existence gets its due in traditional Chinese poetry. Though the poems are actually pretty clearly from a number of hands, the figure of Lady Tzu-ye, a courtesan or female entertainer, was created by tradition to honor the otherwise anonymous creativity to be found in these poems. It is wonderful to be able to close this dark episode of Chinese history, brightened hitherto only by the brilliance of its suffering poets, with celebration. Many of the original poets' euphemisms have lost their meanings in the mist of time. I invite you to try to recover them.

Fought South of the City Wall

Fought south of the city wall:
died north of the ramparts.
Dead on the battleground, unburied:
the crows will feed.
"Say to the crows for us:
enjoy a *warrior*.
Dead on the battleground,
our honor will not bury us,
nor will even our rotting flesh flee.
The waters, deep and rushing, rushing,
among the dark reeds the sun's fallen.
Warriors from horseback; dead in the battle:
warhorses milling and neighing.
We tore up the bridges to build up the barricades,
now no way to flee, north or south:
The ripe grain unreaped; what's for our Lord to eat?
And if he want loyal ministers, whence shall they come?"
"I think of you as my fine ministers:
fine ministers, it is right to rank you so:
Into the dawn light you sallied forth.
With the sunset you did not return."

Going This Path

Going this path, I stumble across the mountain's feet.
My horse gnaws the cypress bark.
I chew the cypress resin.
It doesn't satisfy.
It stays
the pain.

Juan Chi (210–263)

◆ 1

Midnight, can't sleep,
so I sit up, to try my lute.
Curtains catch moonlight
the pure breeze flutters my sleeves.
A lone swan cries: in wilderness,
and flies, crying, to the north woods,
turning, and turning, and gyring there,
sees what?
Loneliness; to be alone so
wounds heart and mind.

◆ 14

Autumn, I know, I fear, it will be cold.
In my bed, I listen to the crickets
beyond my curtains, and I am afraid,
saddened by these little things of nature's.
Gentle, the breeze at my silken sleeves;
the moon: bright as ice . . .
The rooster, in the treetop, crows.
I'll saddle my horse: it's time to go home.

◆ 18

The sun's a chariot in the southeast.
The driver driving, racing, on toward dusk.

Light lingers on the four seas,
then, the sudden darkness reigns.
Dawns, the sun bathes at Hsien-chih.
Evenings, the banks of Meng River welcome the light.
Who yet doubts that brilliant scholars,
enlightened though they be,
once dead, will stay so?
See the peach and the plum in blossom?
Which of them will bloom forever?
A prince among men, can even he
stand free of change?
Alas, he is *one* of, not *one with*, the All.
I stand here, and gaze upon
the evergreens of Mount Chingshan.
They are comfort, solace, for my heart.

◆ 36

Life's hard, some say . . .
Rambling, free, I could run out my days,
here, in my front court, among
these flowering trees, and
in their shade, so lithe and light,
my mind might ponder
                    the *formless void.*
But pacing there I find my heart turns to friends and loved ones,
and all's a sudden dark again.
So I send these poems by the eastward-winging birds . . .
Purging my heart of all the words
that could give form to sadness.

◆ 54

Boasting, even gossiping, you can purge yourself of anger.
But lie, and let it lie, and you'll end up racked with fears . . .
So I climb Puchou Ridge heading northwest, then turn
and look back on the Great Forest of Teng,
hills like bumps on the mountains' backs.
In the old tale ten thousand lifetimes
pass in a dream as water comes to a boil:
a thousand years of risings and fallings.
Who call jade and common stones the same?
I find that I can't keep from weeping.

◆ 69

Just to go among men is difficult for me:
finding a true friend's near a miracle.
When the way is hard, people get tetchy:
that puts the jewel out of reach.
Some hunger to sup from a king's high table:
a bowl of rice is enough for me.
Shall I snatch part of thine to add to my portion?
I'd suffer no less, then, than thee . . .
Advice I might offer'd be taken awry:
I'll keep my mouth shut, save my breath.

◆ 73

Need I learn to fly on horseback?
Tung-ye Chi, fulfilling a fool duke's orders:

even his fine chariot team broke down.
A fish knows to swim deep where a hook's set shallow;
birds, to fly high by a net. I'll drift
with the flow in my skiff, into the endless ocean.
Fish will blow a blanket of bubbles in drying mud
to help each other stay out of the dried-fish shop,
but they'd far rather swim far apart in the sea.
Do you spend much time on making up?
I just try to keep my face clean.
Gods and goddesses? They may indeed live long,
locked in endless trances.

T'ao Ch'ien (365–427)

After the Ancients

Spring's second moon brings timely rain;
thunder rumbles in the east.
Insects stir from secret places.
Grasses, trees and brush spread green.
Wings! Wings everywhere! The new come swallows,
pairs and pairs, within *my* home
find last year's nest still here,
and come, together, to rest, again.
Since you and I were parted, I have
watched the garden gate pile up in leaves.
My heart's no rolling stone.
And yours?
Do you love me still?

From *Drinking Wine, Twenty Poems*

◆ 2

Success and failure? No known address.
This or that goes on, depending on the other.
And who can say if Milord Shao was *happier*
ruling a city, or sacked, his excellent melon patch?
Hot, cold, summer, winter: don't they alternate?
Mayn't a man's way wander on just so?
Yes, those who "get there" know their opportunities . . .
have learned to untie the knots of knowledge.
But was it the *notable* or the *notorious* that *our* Sage spoke of?
The latter *he* called opportunists. Those who get there, doubtless,
know doubt nor care no more. Yet, doubt you not, nor do dead
      generals,
who plotted carefully at what seemed opportune,
and knew naught, right *or* wrong.
If, of a sudden, you're offered fine wine,
let the sun sink. Enjoy it.

◆ 5

I built my hut within man's sphere
and yet can't hear the proclamations of his bustling streets.
You may ask how this can be . . .
When the heart's afar, its place is all its own.

I pluck chrysanthemums in autumn's light beneath my eastern
      hedge,
and gaze toward the mountain, south

where alchemists brew long-life's elixir,
where good farmers go at last to rest,
the distance ever burning in my heart.

In the mountain air: there is good omen of an eve,
as birds fly home, together.

In this, in all of these, there is true meaning . . .
In lusting to find the words . . .
the words' *heart's* lost.

♦ 9

Pure bright, blue, beginning.
Morning, comes a knock.
Ear hears king's summons at the door,
and thus I rush, my shirt on inside-out,
to see unbarred that door, myself.
And who, good man, are you?
It's just some well-intentioned farmer come,
with jug of homebrew held like hat in hand
to pay a call on me because he thinks he sees
me cunning as a child, or, maybe, out of time.
"Your rags, your matted thatch," he says,
"is not your things as makes your *scholar's lofty perch!*
Your whole wide world of gentlefolks agrees!
Won't you too come to help them stir the mud?"
"Deep thanks, old man, for all your thoughts
yet by my nature I must leave alone
that whole wide world, its words (and will).
Though one may surely learn to hold the reins,

to drive the "cart of state," to strive to go
against one's grain is just illusion . . .
come, let us strive to find some joy in sharing of this wine:
my cart will not turn back again."

◆ 11

Confucius loved Yen Hui,
would cite no other, not himself, as *good*.
Of rustic Jung, he said, "This man knows Tao."
Often empty, the one died young.
Always hungry, the other was, even to old age.
Thus they left their names to us:
a life of bitterness, sweet ancient, noble men.
Gone, in death, what was it that they'd known?
To be titled for your nature's good, enough?
Then there was that old man Yang,
who valued his body more than gold,
and spent it, leaving nothing to be buried with.
And is it *wrong* to go naked to the grave?
Perhaps a man, in time, may get beyond the clothing
of conventional ideas . . .

◆ 14

My real friends, Ancient Sages all, approve of what I go for.
Jugs in hand, together, they're here, and perfect.
Brushing up the needles, we sit beneath pines: long-lived, evergreen.
A couple of cups, and we're drunk *again*
(starting over, *got to get it right this time*).

Fathers, elders: random, chaotic talk,
even the horn bowl's lost the order of pouring.
Unconscious, knowing only there's an I, or
is it unenlightened, that's what I don't know?
It might be peaceful to find *things* of value
but no, I can't know even *this* for sure.
When the heart's distant, longing, it's at a loss
for what to keep or where to stay.
Wine puts me right here: so subtle, that flavor.

◆ 16

I was a youth who never spoke about
nor sought connection with the
world of men.
Afloat on the warm bosom of a sea of scripture,
innocent, or arrogant, and without doubt,
at forty, or fifty, sunk, stayed, weaned,
no thing done, or won, unknown.
Finally, firmly, I found virtues in adversity
where, innocent or arrogant, I had found none before.
I found hunger, cold: my found now is all
that changes. This rude hut
is well connected with the heartless
wind, heedless court sunk in imperious weeds,
my ragged wretched robes: I carry on
through endless night.
Morning, but the cock won't crow.
(Thou needst not go.)
No man knows me, no man who offers wine.
Finally, firmly, I hide my feelings, here.

◆ 17

The orchid, hidden, growing, in the court
swallowed in weeds waits wind,
clear wind, pure wind, stripping, burning, bends them low,
and the orchid's seen, above the weedy artemisia.
Aimless motion, the old path lost . . .
If I could keep the way, and bear the truth
I might get through.
When I awake, I'll memorize returning.
When the birds are all gone, a good bow's wasted.

◆ 18

Yang Hsiung, cloud, philosopher, fled court for home,
heart set on meat and wine, but no way to get it,
save, from time to time to
meet, and drink the leas of
Servants of the State,
who came to leave *their* questions all behind.
So the goblet came, and so he left it,
empty. And he found no queries
beyond this solution. Yet
sometimes he would not speak . . .
When but when they asked of sack
and carnage? The good man
answers simply, with his heart. How could he not know
the time to stay,
the Way to go?

Best Option: Stopping Wine

He loves to play beyond the city wall, at home.
He rambles to the mountain's top to idle there alone.
He strives to pass his time beneath shade trees,
or strolls to peaceful music by his gate.
To pluck garden mallows to pleasure the palate,
to have babies to play with: there are
such simple things to please a simple heart . . .
All his life his wine's been his topic . . .
Plots to put it aside now: what pleasure would be left?
When he stops in the evening he finds he can't sleep.
If he stops in the morning, he dares not arise,
first opines he can do it, and then once again,
quick bows to panic when his heart starts to pound.
Seldom has he ever felt desires to punish himself,
and therefore found few reasons to push back his cup.
This day he does, at last, oppugn those errant arguments,
and at dawn's skies' first opening he lays by the jug.
Beginning today at least options appear:
to go perhaps to Paradise, with Spirits to ponder or play,
immune, as time races to plunder the beauty of day . . .
And there, for a thousand forevers to part with the sorrows
of *stopping*.

In Imitation of Old Poems

Someone's come far, far, with the words of the sentence,
the sword of its execution.
A hundred feet up the tower: the view: clean cut, flesh of kings

lost, flowing or flown, off, or, anyway, hidden in the leaves in
all directions, perished.
Sunsets, the tower's home for clouds; mornings, the birds
fly from it. My eyes brim with mountains,
with rivers, flat, plain: alone, lost again
laid waste by the waters, lost in the leaves.
Another season, another time, *merit* named its
warriors, hearts given up on peace, done with
leisure: they strove upon this field.
One: Sunup, sundown: a hundred harvests. Done.
They've gone home together now, drawn on
by martial dirge to Northern Wastes,
there where many nobles lie.
(Birds flee, fish dive deep at that sound.)
The cemetery trees, a hundred pines, and cypress, ever green
until this moment, now, cut down by simple men for fuel.
See? Old mounds do obeisance as the new mounds rise.

Ruined foundations know no masters now. Where
do their shadows wander? Flowers: glory.
Surely swords and halberds found nobility:
surely they've won all the earth
a snail's horns would shade.
Surely, too, (or it might seem)
I might feel pity for their wounds.

Moving House

Once upon a time: I wanted to go live in South Village,
not because of some augery, it was just that I'd heard
good simple men lived there, folks I'd have
been happy to spend time with, mornings and evenings.

Many years, that was what I wanted; now,
today, it's what, hereafter, I shall be *known for* . . .
Well, a simple man's house doesn't have to be big,
all I'll need is a bed, and a mat on a floor is a bed.
Then my neighbors will come visiting, and
we'll talk, we can argue, happy, over other times,
we'll read scarce bits of honest histories, enjoying them, together.
We'll settle *all* the old world's questions, *together.*

Hsieh Ling-yun (385–433)

Passing My Estate at Shih-ning

Bobbed-haired, irksome child, I longed to grow *Upright,*
and find fame for it . . .
But then I found things of this world,
and they held me.
Only yesterday, or it seems so, I let such
honorable ambition go . . .
two dozen years, in fact, the then to now.

Blackened, reamed, worn as a knight would
never be, my nature sullied, I'd betrayed,
forgotten, even the bright broad land itself.
Worn, wasted, wearied, I'm shamed now
by anything upright and firm . . .
But *stupidity* and *sickness* may yet
be my salvation: these have brought me here again
to the very bosom of Silence.
I am empowered by the emblem of a magistrate
to rule "the Blue Sea," but first I'll play king

of my own old hills a while.
Hiking the high places, and the low,
crossing, tracing a winding stream to its source.
Here are cliffs, crags and peaks, and
ranks of ridges, ranges,
like rock islets and bits of sandbar in sea surge.
White clouds wrap dark boulders.
Green bamboo writhe in shamanesses' dances by the stream.

I'll rethatch the roof with the view
of the river's twistings, and raise up
a tower for viewing the peaks.
Then I'll wave farewell to my village folk:
"A three-year term, then I'll return . . .
Plant me graveyard evergreens, and
coffin-wood trees. These
are my last wishes."

Written to Swap, at Tung-yang Creek

I

Pretty! Some man's wife, for sure,
washing those so-white feet in the stream.
And the moon, bright among the clouds:
far, so far away; just out of reach.

II

Pretty! He's some girl's husband . . .
Come on a white skiff adrift on the stream.

"Pray, what be thy purpose here,
as the clouds slip over the moon . . . ?"

Pao Chao (414–466)

Written in Imitation of the Song Called "Hard Traveling"

I

Scribing lines as it goes, water poured on flat ground
runs east or west or north or south as it flows:
human life is also fated. Why then sigh
as you go forward, or melancholy, sit?
Pour wine to fete thyself, raise up the cup
and do not deign to sing "Hard Traveling."
Heart-and-mind; they are not wood-and-stone . . .
How might one not bear pain? And if I know
fear as I stagger on, I'll never deign to speak it.

II

Sir, don't you see? The grass along the riverbank?
In the winter it withers, come spring it springs again
to line all pathways.
Today the sun is set, completely gone, already.
Tomorrow morning won't it rise again?
But when in time shall my way be just so . . .
Once gone, I'm gone forever, banished to the
        Yellow Springs, below.
In human life the woes are many and the satisfactions few:

so seize the moment when you're in your prime.
If one of us achieve a noble aim, the rest may take joy in it.
But best keep cash for wine on the bedside table.
Whether my deeds be scribed on bamboo and silk
is surely beyond my knowing.
Life or death, honor or shame? These I leave to High Heaven.

Songs of Tzu-ye (Lady Midnight's Songs) (5th century?)

Midnight's Song

Nights are long when she can't sleep;
the bright moon glitters like a bangle.
She thinks she hears an answer to a prayer . . .
"Yes . . . ," she murmurs, into empty air.

Quatrains from "Tzu-ye Songs for the Four Seasons"

Spring

Spring groves' blossoms bewitch.
Spring birds sing the heart of sadness.
Spring breeze brings even more of *that certain feeling*:
blowing my gauzy skirt awry.

The plum blossoms have fallen: they're gone,
and the willows, wind's taken them too.
Here I am in the spring of my years!
And no man's thought of taking me.

Summer

Yes, I'm positively thrashing in these sheets . . .
Too hot even for mosquito netting!
But wait, wait a moment, my dear young friend . . .
I haven't even made my face up yet.

Mornings, I climb to the cool of the tower.
Evenings, nap among the orchids by the pool.
In the moonlight, I sit face to face with some flower of manhood,
night after night, gathering the lotus seed.

Heat at the full, silence, no breath of breeze,
even as the summer clouds rise before the setting sun.
Hand in hand, where the leaves are thickest,
we will float my melons, sink your ripe plums.

PART THREE

The Golden Age

Poetry of the T'ang Dynasty (618 C.E.–905 C.E.)

Introduction to Poetry of the T'ang Dynasty

THE T'ANG WAS MOST CERTAINLY THE GOLDEN AGE OF Chinese poetry, as Chinese critics and literary historians have always claimed. And in fact it is clear that China experienced, within the boundaries of the T'ang dynasty, a high level of accomplishment in all areas of human endeavor, from technology to science, from infrastructure (roads, flood control, and irrigation) to the decoration of everyday life (from everyday table ceramics and furniture to public buildings), from community social welfare to community entertainments (commercial storytellers, puppet shows ... missionary preachers of a great variety of religions), and finally to great advancements in all of so-called high culture, including poetry. Perhaps, in the construction of a true golden age, the great arts come last. Art requires, at its foundation, education; starving nations, warring nations, don't spend on education.

The greatest Chinese poets, those whose names are best known in the West—Wang Wei, Li Po, Tu Fu, and a dozen others—come from the middle of the T'ang, after 150 years of what was for the common people perhaps the most peaceful and prosperous time ever known by a human population in recorded history. They were the fruit of a time when education was not just honored but was also supported both by the state and by powerful and wealthy Buddhist churches. They were the product of a state that gave high state employment to poets. They were the product of a state so powerfully constructed that even when the fatal flaw of absolute despotism caused it to topple in midstep, more than a hundred years were required before it well and truly fell . . . and so well-trained poets, born and raised in a happy time, could bring their powers to bear upon war, suffering, injustice, brutality, and death. Finally it is a golden age of poetry to just the degree to which the T'ang's poets vanquished these seemingly perennial demons of humankind.

China was, by 589, more divided by well-defended natural boundaries cloaked in near nation status (one for every defensible river crossing or impassible mountain range) than even early-twentieth-century Europe. In a brilliant stroke of psychological warfare, the leaders of the armies that were to found the Sui Dynasty used a conscious appeal to the people of all these states through Buddhism, the one thing that their masses of ordinary folk held in common. Having achieved peace and unity, those same leaders, through a seemingly systematic program of foreign military aggression and grossly excessive moral corruption at court, squandered all of their political currency in less than forty years and, in 618, handed Li Yuan, first emperor of T'ang, a still more or less united state that was more than ready for new leadership. His son Li Shih-min, who was the power behind the throne from the beginning, settled the question of eventual succession when, with a band of loyal friends, he ambushed and killed his brother and set his father aside. China's Golden Age was off and flapping on the dark leather wings of realpolitik. Strange as it might seem after this little summary, in the early years of T'ang reign Taoism was the state ideology (the family name was Li, a very common one in China, but also coincidentally the surname of the legendary founder of Taoism, Lao Tzu) . . . apparently Buddhism's attachment to the Sui had ruined its fragrance, and Confucian scholars had yet to recover credibility after their centuries-long collaboration with evil rulers.

After a period of a little over sixty years, during which the T'ang made great strides in reconsolidating the wealth and power squandered by the Sui, the T'ang throne was usurped by a woman, Wu Tzu-t'ian, who ruled with extraordinary vigor and insight for twenty years. She was succeeded by perhaps the most famous of all Chinese emperors, Hsuan Tsung, also known and loved by the popular title Ming Huang, "the brilliant emperor"; he was indeed brilliant (maybe even as brilliant as Wu Tzu-t'ian), until senility combined with absolute power to let him nearly topple the dynasty in the middle of the eighth century. The imperial favorite of that moment, Yang Kuei-fei, helped a Turkish (mercenary) general capture the imperial capital and begin a rebellion that, despite some more strong leadership from the amazingly strong Li family line, never quite ended before the end of the dynasty in 906.

Amid these fascinating human dramas extraordinary cultural achievements marked every year of the T'ang, as if the peach trees of the utopian dreams of T'ao Ch'ien were blossoming and bearing fruit in every orchard in the land. Major advances took place in every field, from mathematics and engineering to finance and education. Confucian thought flourished, eventually recovering its position as the dominant state ideology, while Buddhism also flourished and grew strong, forming religious communities and providing social institutions, among them hospitals, orphanages, and old folks' homes, which had never existed before. Education was fostered by Buddhist churches as well as by the state. Music and drama made major strides under imperial patronage, and painting and poetry both began to explore new avenues of expression and reached new heights in already traditional forms. The development of Buddhist thought and institutions in the T'ang is another area that will easily yield the interested reader a lifetime of interesting reading.

Finally, the imperial civil service examination system, begun in a rudimentary fashion in around 100 B.C.E., was strongly promoted by the usurping Empress Wu and then, amazing as it seems, was retained and even given an increasing role in the choosing of government officials of all sorts under the leadership of the great Ming Huang. The principle of meritocracy was strong in the Confucianism of Confucius and Mencius, so strong that it was enshrined in the central myth of Chinese culture, the story of

Yao and Shun, the "emperors" who shunned their own offspring and chose instead the most able men of the empire as their successors. From the T'ang on, whenever the government itself was strong enough to enforce "civil" administration, the examinations made sure that most qualified men (of course women were excluded, even during the reign of Empress Wu) found employment *in government*. The Jesuits of Enlightenment Europe who saw this system at work in China in the Ming thought that its institution in Europe might head off the revolutions that aristocratic monopolization of governmental power did indeed play a role in igniting.

For the poetry enthusiast, the greatest "invention" of the T'ang was neither Buddhism nor the examination system, though poetic innovations may have had something to do with the success of both. Two types of poetry are identified particularly with the T'ang. The first, *lu-shih*, or "regulated verse," was used in the highest level of the most important and prestigious of the civil service examinations. The other type, *chueh chu*, has been translated a number of ways but means simply a four-line verse, or quatrain. Since the economical qualities of the Chinese writing system allow these quatrains to be packed with meaning, my translations of them are sometimes driven beyond four lines of English.

Regulated verse was actually "invented" by Shen Yueh (441–515), a Buddhist-inspired scholar-official who was, of course, also a poet. He had been attempting to discover a means of translating into Chinese the supernaturally powerful Sanskrit prayers without losing the magical power of the sounds of the mantras, which were (and are) believed to call spirit beings to the aid of tantric Buddhist meditators. When his spiritual labors led to discoveries about the fundamental nature of *euphony* in the Chinese spoken language, such was the strength of the indigenous concept of *wen* for Shen Yueh that, devout Buddhist though he was, he turned with passion from his religion back to *poetry* and formulated extremely elaborate rules for the creation of euphonious poetry. To the ears of fellow poets, his formulas made perfect sense, and from the beginning of the eighth century until the beginning of the twentieth, when classical Chinese itself went out of fashion, no man who couldn't write a proper piece of regulated verse would be considered a proper gentleman. Of course, a surpassingly beautiful piece of "verse" and a good poem don't necessarily have much in common.

The standard eight-line regulated verse was used in the T'ang (and during some periods of later dynasties) as the basis of the literary examinations, by far the most prestigious of the several kinds of exams. While even lovers of Chinese poetry might be tempted to erupt in howls of derision at the thought of high government positions being granted to the best writers of greeting-card verses or "silly love songs," in fact absolute technical perfection in the execution of the formal rules of versification was only the slightest of the demands of the examination poem. The topic of the poem generally required that the examination candidate demonstrate perfect memorization of the Confucian Classics, later historical and poetic works, and scholarly commentaries on all of them, as well as mastery of rhetoric and character etymology. An examination poem must "seem" like a silly love song while permitting a deep reading in which the "poet" candidate shows diplomatic skills in the presentation of delicate policy issues. Simply because we don't have the resources to tie the poems to their topical issues, most examination poems from the T'ang are untranslatable. Fresh from the brush of the poet they were doubtless exciting reading, providing an excellent index not just of the candidate's general learning and communications skills but of his intellectual and social sophistication and mastery of the diplomatic arts. A regulated verse on a well-conceived topic was an efficient way to find young men who could learn to govern: *chun tzu*.

Outside the examination system, the regulated form was used mainly for so-called occasional verse. Poetry was a part of every social occasion in China, and not just among the elite: for every young man who passed the examination there were literally thousands who began the education process and advanced far enough in it to develop a love of both the subject matter and the formal means. But it remains true that though even a wild man like Li Po wrote more than a few regulated verses (to prove he could?), most poets wrote most of their poems in less technically demanding forms. The *yueh-fu*, or old-style verse, flourished even during the period of greatest popularity of the regulated verse, and survived it.

The quatrain, sometimes created out of a variety of cuttings and pastings from the lines prescribed for the regulated verse, and sometimes just four lines of five- or seven-character *yueh-fu*, set the poet completely free. In some hands the quatrain was the perfect vehicle for a simple "snapshot" of a beautiful vista. In other hands it was used to provide a flash of pure spiritual insight.

It was a long period, the temporal home of a "Golden Age," and T'ang was home to hundreds of skillful and inspired poets. There are all sorts of men: Ch'en Tzu-ang served the usurper Empress Wu; Meng Hao-jan, though he was a close friend of influential poets like Wang Wei and Li Po, failed the Exams and lived out his life in seclusion. Po Chu-i, made a blazing early reputation for himself with a poem that pandered to the Imperial family's deep embarrassment about the senile Hsuan Tsung's besotted love for his concubine Yang Kuei-fei, and redeemed himself in later life, heading, along with his close friend the poet Yuan Chen, a movement of poets who wrote poems committed to the cause of social justice, poems written in a language that could be understood when read aloud to ordinary folk. The list goes on and on . . . Including the six Zen poets grouped, without regard to chronology, at the end of the selection, there are thirty poets in this section of the anthology. A few of the poets I have selected for inclusion here are separated from oblivion by a single extant poem. In the twenty years since I translated the poem by Wang Han (p. 83), I have been able to find no more about him than the poem and the poet's name and dates, and I'm left to wonder whether he was a grizzled veteran or an imaginative courtier. And there are a few poets represented here by more than a dozen poems, and for whom there exists enough biographical material for a book or two. There is no reason to bother about assigning a label like "best" from among these poets, but it's something we do, and something the Chinese do as well, though it appears they do it with a bit more of a sense of humor.

It comes down, first, to three . . . No one would doubt that Wang Wei, Li Po, and Tu Fu are in some perhaps indefinable way "better" than each and all of the other poets. The three are very different. Wang Wei was an aristocrat, born with a silver writing brush in his mouth. Of all the privileged among the Chinese poets of all periods of her history, Wang Wei made best use of his privilege. He was a musician of surpassing skill and a landscape painter so innovative that he can be said to have changed landscape painting from his time forward. He was also a patron of poets (he probably saved Li Po from execution), and, not least, patron of the Southern School of Zen Buddhism, the school from which arose both the Rinzai and the Soto schools known to modern scholars and practitioners alike. Most importantly, he was a poet of consummate skill. There is no doubt that Wang Wei's *chueh chu*, his quatrains, are somehow something other than anyone else's. Su Shih, the great Sung poet, said that Wang Wei's poems are paintings, and his paintings, poems. More than a thousand years of readers have agreed. But there is more. Wang Wei's readers almost invariably find themselves *inside* his poems. Something is happening here, and I don't know what it is, except that I'm in the presence of surpassing poetic genius.

And yet Wang Wei doesn't even get mentioned as *best* poet.

Li Po is the god of poetry. He called himself only the god of wine, and refused on the grounds of his *superiority* to answer a call from his Emperor. His poetry shows us, almost always, a person who is outside the world we live in, looking even farther outward at things we can't even imagine. He dances with the moon and his shadow (p. 92), making a three that's not a crowd. He meditates upon a mountain (p. 90) until he and the mountain are One. And yet he is the absolute master of the description of human intimacy. It seems almost impossible that the delicate picture of a young love growing into maturity in "The Ballad of Ch'ang-kan" (pp. 95–96) should have been written by a swashbuckling drunkard, and no less that that poet should also be in communication with Ch'u Yuan and his Fisherman (p. 93). It's more understandable to discover in "Drinking with a Hermit Friend in the Mountains" (p. 90) that in a single excellent, immortal quatrain this man has repeated himself three times in a single line, and then stolen a line from a history book he's just been reading (or has memorized) almost word for word! There is, after all, the saying that all poets borrow, great poets steal. The vitality of a giant and the delicacy of a fairy prince. A freedom beyond most imaginations, and a rigorous *artistic* discipline that is, perhaps, even harder to imagine. No mere *man* could write so: so he is no man, but the spirit, the earthly presence, of the elemental power that is poetry.

Leaving room for another best poet: the best human poet, Tu Fu.

He loves his wife. He loves his children. He loves his ruler as a symbol of good government, and when that symbol fails, he shows his love for the people who are the purpose of good government. He loves wine, perhaps like T'ao Ch'ien, whose work he admires, he finds drinking and drunkenness interesting symbols, for both spiritual enlightenment and the rewards of power, sometimes simultaneously . . . He is without question the absolute, hands down, master of regulated verse. But he is not "formalist."

Form is his servant, never his master. He loves and feels ever anxious about Li Po. Li Po loves him, teasing him for his discipline as he admires the poetic results. How to say it? He combines disciplined artistry with a simple humanity and deep commitment to human values, creating poems that show universal truths. To put it simply, Tu Fu is the ultimate embodiment of *wen*.

If you disagree with this high assessment of Tu Fu, you will find yourself in pretty good company. Li Po and Tu Fu both looked with favor upon T'ao Ch'ien. It was several centuries before anyone took Tu Fu seriously. Many later poets and readers favored Su Tung-p'o of the Sung Dynasty. But for the limitations of her life that may have taken some themes from her, Li Ch'ing-chao might have a serious following. Perhaps the best of the best lies unread in a library of Ming or even Ch'ing dynasty poets, presently condemned, without a fair reading, as a mere imitator, as many Ming and Ch'ing poets truly were. Ah, for another lifetime to spend reading poetry!

Ch'en Tzu-ang (661–702)

Climbing the Terrace of Yu-chou

Before, I cannot see the men of old.
Beyond, can't see the men to come.
Ponder the infinite, Heaven and Earth.
Alone, confused, I melt to tears.

Chang Chiu-ling (678–740)

"Since you, my lord, left me"

Since you, my lord, left me,
all my labors . . . left undone.
Thinking of you, I am like the full moon;
night by night, my bright luster wanes.

Wang Han (687–726)

Song of Liang-chou

Good wine of the grape: cup of night's brightness.
To drink to the *P'i-p'a*, rushing on horseback.
If I fall, drunk, upon this sandy field, don't laugh.
From all these frontier wars, how many have returned?

Meng Hao-jan (689–740)

Passing the Night on the Chien-te River

My boat moored by misty isle,
sun sets, while a traveler's grief rises.
Above vast plain, sky lowers among the trees.
In the limpid stream, the moon moves close.

Spring Morning

Spring, napped, unconscious of the dawn.
Everywhere, birdsong.
Night sounded, wind, and rain.
How many petals, now, are fallen?

Master I's Chamber in the Ta-yu Temple

I-kung's place to meditate:
this hut, in empty grove.
Outside the door, a pretty peak.
Beyond the stairs, deep valleys.
Sunset confused in footprints of the rain.
Blue of the void in the shade of the court.
Look, and see: the lotus blossom's purity.
Know, thus: nothing tainted *that* man's heart.

Wang Ch'ang-ling (698–765)

Palace Lament

Young wife in her chamber, so innocent of grief.
Spring morn adorned, she climbs blue tower,
where sudden she sees, along the lane, the willow's colors,
and sorrows, now, she sent him off, in search of honors.

Wang Wei (701–761)

Bamboo Pavilion

I sit alone among the tallest of the tall bamboo,
pluck the lute, and whistle melodies, again.
This deep grove's unknown to other men.
Bright moon, when it comes: we shine together.

Deer Park

Empty mountain, none to be seen.
Listen close and all you'll hear's
the birdsong sound of human language.
Sun's come into this deep grove,
beginning again, it writes on gray-green lichen, upon stone.

In the Mountains

Ching gorge: the white rocks jut.
Cold sky: red leaves grow few.
The mountain road is bright, no rain.
Just azure emptiness: that wets the cloak.

Birdsong Torrent

The man at his ease: the cassia flowers falling.
Night quiet: spring mountain empty.
Moonrise: shocks the mountain birds.
Sometimes you'll hear their cries, among spring's torrents.

Dike of the Cormorants

Sudden, plunged down among red lotus,
again, he soars above the bright strand.
Alone, there standing: see the wings spread,
and the fish in his beak, on the floating log.

Lake Yi

With flute song, to the shore:
the setting sun, and I see you off.
On the lake, you looked back once:
white cloud, embracing the green mountains.

In Retirement at Chung-nan Mountain

To middle age I loved the Tao:
late now, I lodge on South Mountain
and when I'm up to it, I always go alone.
All this beauty, mine, in vain, alone.
All my triumphs, self-knowledge: *empty*.
Walking gets me *where* the waters narrow.
Sitting, I can see to *when* the clouds arise.
But if I should meet up with any old woodsman,
we'll chatter and giggle with no thought of home.

Mount Chung-nan

Great primordial mountain, residing by
the star we know as Heaven's Capital,
and linked, by range on range of peaks, to the sea.
White clouds, when I look back, close in.
Blue mists, as I enter them, are gone.
The pivot of the constellations' turning:
the shaded gorge and sun-drenched ridge defining yin and yang.
I try to find a place to stay here,
across the stream, calling to the woodcutter.

Autumn Mountain Evening

Empty mountain, after rain,
the air of nightfall come to autumn.

Bright moon: among the pines, it's shining.
Pure spring: over the rocks, it runs.
Bamboo rustles as the washing maids wend homeward,
and lotus stir as the fishermen's craft do too.
If you will, you may still find spring's fragrances.
You too, my gentle friend, may stay.

Mission to the Frontier

In a single cart, finding the way to the frontier,
beyond Ch'u-yan, past conquered states,
wandering grass beyond our borders:
a wild goose against this alien sky.
Vast desert! Lone spire of smoke stands straight.
Long dry river, setting sun rolls round.
At Desolation Pass we met a patrol,
"Headquarters camp's at Swallow Mountain."

Passing the Temple of Gathered Fragrance

Where *is* the Temple of Gathered Fragrance?
Just how many *li* away among those cloudy peaks?
Among the ancient trees, no paths for men.
Deep in the mountains, where *is* that bell?
The sound of the welling spring
is caught in the throat of the stony stream.
Blanched in sere sunlight
the pines look colder still.
In the thin winter dusk, by the dry lake's edge,
I sit in meditation, taming poison dragons.

To Magistrate Chang

Late, I love only quiet;
things of the world no longer concern me.
Looking back, I've never known a better policy
than this: returning to my grove.
Pine breezes: loosen my robe.
Mountain moon: playing on my lute.
Sir, you ask guidance, *rules* for success and failure:
the fisherman's song strikes deep up the cove.

Li Po (701–762)

Down to Chiang-ling

Morning, from the White Emperor City,
among the many colored clouds . . .
And then, a thousand *li* in a single day, to Chiang-ling.
From both banks, the apes' cries, unceasing.
This little boat has *gone beyond* ten thousand mountain ranges.

Seeing Off Meng Hao-jan at the Pavilion of the Yellow Crane

Old friend, you said your good-byes to the west from this pavilion.
Through misted blossoms in the third month, you'll go down to
     Yangchou.
Your lonely sail, a distant shadow, across the blue of mountains.
All I can see, the Long River, flowing, to the edge of the heavens.

East Mountain

I love East Mountain's music.
I could stay a thousand years here or just never leave.
I'd wave my dancing sleeve,
and sweep clean the Mountain of the Five-Trunked Pine.

Drinking with a Hermit Friend in the Mountains

Together, we drink: mountain flowers, opening.
A cup, a cup, and then, to *begin again*, another cup!
I'm drunk, would sleep . . . you'd better go.
Tomorrow, come again, with your lute, if you will.

Sitting at Reverence Mountain

The flocks have flown high up and gone.
A single cloud fades into emptiness.
In meditation, endlessly, we two.
Then: only the Mountain of Reverence.

Thoughts of a Quiet Night

Before the bed, bright moonlight.
I took it for frost on the ground.
I raised my head to dream upon that moon,
then bowed my head, lost, in thoughts of home.

Jade Stairs Lament

Jade steps grow white dew.
Night, late, chills silken hose.
So let the crystal curtain fall . . .
In the tinkling, gaze upon so many autumn moons.

At Ch'iu-pu Lake

White hair! Three thousand yards of it.
And a sadness, a sorrow, as long.
I don't understand. Where did my bright mirror
find all this autumn frost?

Ballad of the Voyager

Ocean voyager, on heaven's winds,
in his ship, far wandering . . .
Like a bird, among the clouds,
gone, he will leave no trace.

Searching for Master Yung

So many cliffs, jade blue to scour the sky,
I've rambled, years uncounted,
brushing aside the clouds, to seek to ask the Ancient Way,
or maybe leaned against a tree to listen to a stream flow.
Among sun-warmed blossoms, the blue ox sleeps.

In the tall pines, the white crane naps.
Words came to me, with the river sunset:
alone, I came down, through the cold mist.

Seeing Off a Friend

Green mountains draw a line beyond the Northern Rampart.
White Water curls around the Eastern Wall.
This place? Good as any for a parting . . .
Ahead just the lonely briars where you'll march ten thousand *li*.
Floating clouds: the traveler's ambition.
Falling sun: your old friend's feelings.
We touch hands, and now you go.
Muffled sighs, and the post horses, neighing.

Drinking under the Moon

Among the flowers, a jug of wine.
Drinking alone, without companion.
I raise the cup, invite bright moon,
and my shadow; that makes three.
The moon knows nothing of drinking.
My shadow merely follows me.
But I'll play with moon and shadow,
joyful, till spring ends.
I sing as the moon dances.
I dance as my shadow tumbles.
Sober, when we found our joy.
Drunk, each goes his way.
Forever bound, to ramble free,
to meet again, in the River of Stars.

Ancient Air

I climbed high, to gaze upon the sea:
Heaven and Earth, so vast, so vast.
Frost clothes all things in autumn;
winds waft, the broad wastes cold.
Glory, splendor; always, ever,
eastward, seaward, flowing streams;
this world's affairs, just waves.
White sun covered, its dying rays,
the floating clouds, no resting place.
In lofty *wu-t'ung* trees nest lowly finches.
Down among the thorny brush the phoenix perches.
All that's left, to go home again,
hand on my sword I sing, "The Going's Hard."

Bathing

If it's perfumed, don't brush your cap.
Fragrant of orchid, don't shake your gown.
This world hates a thing too pure.
Those who know will hide their light.
At Ts'ang-lang dwells a fisherman:
"You and I, let us go home together."

A Farewell Banquet for My Uncle, the Revisor Yun, at the Pavilion of Hsieh T'iao

It's broken faith and gone, has yesterday: I couldn't keep it.
Tormenting me, my heart, today, too full of sorrow.

High wind sees off the autumn's geese,
on their journey of ten thousand *li*.

Facing all this, it's fitting we should drink upon the high pavilion.
Immortal letters, bones of the great age of Chien-an,
here Hsieh T'iao is clearly heard again.
All embracing, his thoughts fly free,
mount to blue heaven, caress the bright moon . . .

I grasp the sword and strike the water, still the water, flows.
Raise the cup to drown my grief, grief only grows.
Live as men live in this world, and find no satisfactions:
in the bright dawning, hair unbound, to float free in the skiff . . .

Ancient Air

Westward over Lotus Mountain . . .
Afar, far off: Bright Star!
Hibiscus blooms in her white hand,
with airy step she climbs to the realm of Great Purity.
Robed in rainbows, trailing a broad sash,
floating above as she brushes the heavenly stairs,
and invites me to mount the Cloud Terrace,
there to salute the immortal Wei Shu-ch'ing.
Ravished, mad, I go with her,
upon a swan to reach the Purple Vault.
There I looked down, on Loyang's waters:
vast sea of barbarian soldiers marching,
fresh blood spattered on the grasses of the wilds.
Wolves, with men's hats on their heads.

Ballad of Ch'ang-kan

My hair barely covered my forehead then.
My play was plucking flowers by the gate.
You would come on your bamboo horse,
riding circles round my bench, and pitching green plums.
Growing up together here, in Ch'ang-kan,
two little ones; no thought of what would come.
At fourteen I became your wife,
blushing and timid, unable to smile,
bowing my head, face to dark wall.
You called a thousand times before I answered.
At fifteen I carefully made up my face,
and swore that our dust and ashes should be one,
swore I'd keep faith like "the Man at the Pillar."
How could I know I'd "climb the Watchtower" in fact?
For when I was sixteen you journeyed far,
to Chü-t'ang Gorge, by Yan-yü Rocks.
In the fifth month, there is no way through,
there where the apes call, mournful to the heavens.

By the gate, the footprints that you left,
each one has grown green with moss,
so deep, I have not swept them.
The falling leaves, the autumn's wind is early,
October's butterflies already come,
in pairs to fly above the western garden's grass,
wounding the heart of the wife who waits,
sitting in sadness, fair face growing old.
Sooner or later, you'll come down from San-pa.
Send me a letter, let me know.

I'll come out to welcome you, no matter how far,
all the way to Long Wind Sands . . .

Ancient Air

Moon's tint can't be swept away;
the traveler's grief? There's no way to say it.
White dew proclaims from autumn robes.
Fireflies flit above the grasses.
Sun and moon are in the end extinguished;
Heaven and Earth, just so, will rot away.
A cricket cries in the green pine tree
he'll never see grow old.
Potions of long life can only fool the vulgar;
the blind find all discernment hard.
You'll never live to be a thousand,
and early anguish only leads to early death.
Drink deep, and dwell within the cup.
Conceal yourself there: you are your only treasure.

To the Tune of P'u-sa-man

Grove on the plain, sun, leaves, water, all interwoven in
    the mist.
The belt of cold mountains, heart-wounding green.
Sunset colors the high pavilion.
Someone sits there grieving,
on the jade stairs, waits, in vain.
Night birds flying, hastening home.
And how goes my way from here?

Inns, and inns,
inns and waystations.

Drinking Alone beneath the Moon II

If Heaven didn't love Wine,
there wouldn't be a Wine Star in Heaven.
If Earth didn't love wine,
there wouldn't be a Wine Spring on Earth.
Since Heaven and Earth both clearly love Wine,
how dare a mere drinking Man fear reproof?
The clear wine, I hear
will make you a Sage,
and some say the muddy's
the way to fathoming true wisdom.
Since the Sage and the Wise were both drinkers,
what need have I to search for some Immortal Spirit?
Three cups: I break on through to the *Great Way*,
A jar full and I am *Nature, Naturing!*
If you want what's worth getting: wine's where it is.
Nothing doing for the stories of the sober . . .

Ancient Air

Deep in the gorgeous gloom the lotus grows,
to blossom fresh upon the morning air.
Its petals cover even the clarity of autumn's flow,
its leaves spreading, blue smoke there.
But it's in vain, this beauty that would overwhelm the world.
Who sees it? Who will say he saw?

And in its time the frost will come, chilling,
its deep red will wither, and its fragrance fade.
Poor choice it's made of where to put its roots.
It would be seen to more advantage in a garden pond.

Ruins: The Ku-su Palace

The garden's desert, crumbling walls, as willows green again.
Even the sweet song of spring's a lament.
Nothing of what was, but the moon above the river,
moon that shone on a pretty face in the palace of the king of Wu.

Ruins: The Capital of Yueh

Kou Chien returned here, triumphant.
He had destroyed Yueh's always enemy, the state of Wu.
Loyal warriors streamed home, armor all draped in Wu brocades
and court ladies waited, thronging, all the flowers of spring.
Now all: a covey of partridges, flushed, fly into the twilight.

Liu Ch'ang-ch'ing (709–785?)

Searching for the Taoist Monk Ch'ang at South Creek

His way, crossed by many lesser paths,
the moss, by sandal tracks.
White clouds lean, at rest on the silent island.
Fragrant grasses bar the idle gate.

Rain past, look: see clear, the color of the pines.
Out along the mountain, to the source,
flowers in the stream reveal Ch'an's meaning.
Face to face, and all words gone.

Tu Fu (712–770)

Moonlight Night

Moon of this night, in Fu-chou,
alone in your chamber you gaze.
Here, far away, I think of the children,
too young to remember Longpeace . . .
Fragrant mist, moist cloud of your hair.
In that clear light, your arms jade cool.
When, again to lean together, by your curtain there,
alight alike, until our tears have dried.

Wayfarer's Night

Sleep? And how could I?
This autumn night, unwilling to grow bright,
the curtain rolled, these fragments of moon shadow,
I'm pillowed high up: far off: the river sounds.
My stupid schemes: no clothes, no food.
The road run out, my life depends on old acquaintances.
My old wife wrote, filled many pages
that I should know she waits
and longs for my return.

Captive Spring

The nation is sundered; the mountains, the rivers, remain.
In the city, spring; trees and grasses, flourishing.
Touched by times passing, flowers drip my tears.
Pained at this separation, birds jar the heart.
Beacons of war have burned a full three months.
A note from home? I'd give a thousand gold for one.
My white hair, scratched ever thinner,
not enough left now for a hatpin.

House Cricket

House cricket . . .
Trifling thing,
and yet how his mournful song moves us.
Out in the grass his cry was a tremble,
but now he trills beneath our bed, to share his sorrow.
I lie still beside you, finding no release:
you, old wife, you suffer quiet through till dawn.
The song of our selves may move us, restless,
through long nights. The cricket's song of autumn
holds us still.

Village by the River

Clear stream meanders by this hamlet, flowing.
Long summer days, at River Village, everything is ease.
Coming, going, as they please, the pairs of swallows soaring.

Mated, close, the gulls float with the stream.
My old wife draws a board for chess.
My son bends pins for fishhooks.
I'm often sick, but I can find good herbs.
What, beyond this, could a simple man ask?

Poem for Tso on His Return to the Mountains

"White dew," we call the season when the yellow millet ripens,
ready for the sharing of an ancient promise.
It must already be ground fine.
It seems, may be, I'm just a little late arriving.
The flavor's *really* not as fine as golden aster.
It's tasty, nonetheless, flavored with green mallow.
Old time old man's food . . .
Just the thought, and my mouth waters.

Song of the Bound Chickens

The little bond-slave binds our chickens for the market,
and the chickens being bound begin to struggle and proclaim.
The *family's* up in arms because the chickens eat the ants,
never thinking that the market means the pot,
as far as chickens are concerned.
Ants, chickens: Man, which most deserves concern?
I told the bondman to unbind them.
No end here to the wars of ants and chickens.
I lean in this high place, eyes fixed
to the cold flow, to the River.

Facing Snow

Wailing war, so many fine young ghosts:
chanting sadness, one poor lame old man.
A chaos of clouds droops into the sunset:
a rush of snowflakes dances, whirling in the wind.
The wine pot's pushed aside, cup empty of its green:
the stove abides, there coals glow red.
No news from anywhere gets through.
Sadness sits, to draft a letter
into emptiness.

Thinking of My Little Boy

Pony Boy, it's spring, and we're still parted.
The orioles sing, as if to warm away our troubles.
Parted from you: surprised as your birthday passes,
not a one to brag to of the clever things you do.
Water falls, there, by the empty mountain road,
by bramble gate, at Ancient Trees, the village where you dwell.
I think of you, and sleep's the only antidote for grief.
I toast my back, bent, bowed,
beneath the smiling sunlight on the porch.

Remembering

"Pony Boy's a good boy," you'd say,
two years ago, when you learned to talk.
You asked, and learned, all my guest's names,
and even chanted your old father's poems.

In these disordered times, I ache at your smallness.
In a poor home, at least you know a mother's love.
There's no way now to lead you to a safe retreat,
nor even to know if this letter will get through.
Heaven and Earth are filled with martial banners.
Mountains and rivers grieve to war horn's moan.
Just let me return, and find you safe:
from that day forth,
                    I'll be a long time leaving.

Tsung-wu's Birthday

This little boy, when did we meet?
High autumn, on this very day your birth.
And from the time I wrote of you from the capital,
your name's been linked with mine in fame.
It's poetry's profession of this house.
Let others hand down love for lesser things.
For you, a thorough knowledge
of the essence of the Wen Hsüan,
and an end to searching after "pretty" things.
I'm fading fast, even as the feast begins:
I list to one side, can't sit upright.
Sunset's clouds break all apart.
Drop by drop I'll pour them out, with drunken dignity.

To Show to Tsung-wu on New Year's Day

You exclaim, that my hand should tremble.
I smile, that your young frame grows strong.

We've met this first moon many places,
scattered, chips on water, far from home.
And though the family's poor as fallen leaves,
still, here's cypress wine to greet the New Year.
And thought I'm frail and sick, there's study too.
Take my instruction, son.
Though I'm shamed so little fame crowns this white head,
I can still build an essay, still write a poem . . .
Your toast to long life is all the more worth answering.
Yet, when I think of my brother,
gone, east of the river, there . . .
Though loud and high I sing,
the only lines that I can make are lines of tears.

Gone by Myself to the Riverbank, in Search of a Flower
(Seven quatrains)

I

By the river, by the flowers, tried.
If I couldn't complain I'd go crazy.
I searched for Hu-ssu Jung, my jug mate:
He's still out drinking! A full ten days
he's left *his own* bed empty.

II

Secret blossoms, buds in dishabille: awesome
by the river. I go listing, reeling, really

afraid of spring. With poems and wine I can endure
the urge: the urge remains. No need yet
for help, *this* old white head.

III

Deep river, stillness of bamboo, two or three homes.
Busybody blossoms blush, sunset
on white, blooming. I know one way
to settle with the blaze of spring.
Go find the wine, and drink the sun down.

IV

Gaze east: the little hamlet, flowers fill the mist.
That house, Hundred Blossoms Hall's high up, the more's
temptation. But who would bring *me* wine, unstop
the bottle there. Call forth a beauty, to dance, before the couch.

V

By the grave of the abbot, Huang, east
of the river, in spring's bright,
lazy, caged. Leaning on light breeze,
the peach, a single banner branch
opens on her own. You may love the deep fresh red:
I love the faded better.

VI

At the house of the madam, Huang,
flowers fill the well-worn paths.
A thousand buds, ten thousand blossoms
weigh branches down. Full of joy
some playful butterfly may dance.
Full of herself, some pretty oriole gives voice.

VII

If I couldn't see the flowers, I'd
prefer to die. My only fear's
that when they're gone, my own life too
will hurry on. How easily, too easily
these flighty blossoms fall. O gentle buds:
consult with me, to part more carefully.

Quatrain

At riverside, spring's celebration
done. I turn to find bright
battle flags. Wind rising. Spring.
The city's dusk.
Watchtowers, fife and drum: spring's
grief again.

Meandering Stream I

When one petal flies, spring's a diminished thing:
wind wafts away ten thousand more, to grieve me.

I will watch what will be gone, these flowers, pass the eye,
and I won't stint to stanch my wounds:
good wine shall pass these lips.
In small pavilions by the stream, kingfishers build their nests.
In the high tombs by the park, the unicorns are sleeping.
See clear the *Rule of Things*, and take your pleasure:
what use to be all bound up in thoughts of fame.

Meandering Stream II

On the way home from court each morning,
I'm pawning off my spring robes
and every day, I stay by the stream until
I'm almost too drunk to go home.
Wine debts are common; even I've got a few.
We're supposed to live threescore and ten; not many do.
Delving the blossoms, the butterfly,
I peer at him as he peers so deep within.
Dinting the water, the dragonflies,
touching, so lightly as they fly.
They say that even wind and light pass on,
are gone together with the stream.
Given, then, this small reward, I have no quarrel.

Facing My Wine at Meandering Stream

Outside the park, beside the stream, I might sit forever.
The crystal palaces are wrapped in chilly mist.
Peach blossoms wait, then follow willow's flowers, falling.
The brown birds go, with the white birds, flying.
I get drunk, stay drunk; all *Righteous* men reject me.

I'm late to court, and it's my due, that all *True* Men ignore me.
It's only petty greed makes paradise so far . . .
And I'm old, and worn with sorrow, and still here.

Spring, Overnight in the Chancellery

The flowers hidden, by the palace walls, sun sets.
Songs sob of autumn, as the birds fly off to roost.
Stars lower near the doors of common folk.
The moon goes visiting among the people of the palace.
Sleepless, I hear the turn of golden keys,
and in the wind chimes find the jingling pendants of
    my horse.
At morning Audience I have words that must be said:
I ask myself again, if I should know, should I pretend
    to know,
        "How goes the night?"

The Flowered Duck

O Flowered Duck, you're spotted, but not stained.
Before the stairs each day, you, stately, waddle by.
The plumage of your wings proclaims your independence:
black and white (and nothing in between) too clearly seen.
Don't you know the others are all jealous?
Careful not to startle watching eyes.
You've got your share of rice and millet.
Make up your mind: don't be the first to quack.

Beginning of Winter

I sag with age: these martial robes are tight.
Coming home, cold's colors deepen.
Fishing boats work up the rushing stream.
A hunter's fire marks the high-perched grove.
Long as there's sun, I drink by leisure's pools.
When sorrows come, I'll chant of ancient heroes.
Spears and halberds still can't be laid by.
To stay, or to serve, which way
does the heart go from here?

Day after the Beginning of Autumn

The sun, the moon, they're unforgiving:
once again two seasons, last night, shared a boundary . . .
Dark cicadas, ceaseless, cry . . .
Autumn's swallows, guests, prepare to go.
All my life I've sworn to walk alone,
heart bound to disappointments, this half a hundred years.
To quit, or hold this post, it's up to me;
what is it binds, what jails this body here?

Gazing on the Wasteland

Clear autumn: gaze no end.
Far, far off, rise towers of shadow.
Distant waters, pure as sky.
The lonely city deep in smoky clouds.

Leaves few, the more winds fell,
in mountain's coils, sun sinking,
the single crane flies home: too late.
Dusk's ravens fill the grove.

Lament for Ch'en-t'ao

First month of winter, ten counties' gentle youths'
blood serves for water in the Ch'en-t'ao swamps.
Broad wilds, clear skies: no sounds of battle now.
Forty thousand volunteers, in one day, dead.
Then the Tartars returned, arrows bathed in blood,
still baying their barbarous songs as they drank in the markets.
The people turned away, standing weeping, facing north,
day and night their single prayer: our army may return.

The Press-Gang at Shih-hao Village

At evening, I found lodging in Shih-hao.
That night a press-gang came for men.
An old man jumped the wall,
while his wife went through the gate to meet them.
The officer cursed, so full of anger.
The old woman cried, so bitterly.
Then I heard her approach him and speak:
"Our three sons went off in defense of Ye-ch'eng,
now one has sent a letter home,
to tell us that the other two are slain.
He who remains yet clings to life.
They who have died are gone forever.

At home here there is no one
but a grandson at the breast,
and his mother, not yet able to leave him.
And anyway, she's not a whole skirt to put on . . .
This old one, though her strength is ebbing,
begs you, sir, to let her come tonight,
to answer the draft for Ho-yang.
I might still help to cook the morning meal."
Night lengthened, the voices died away,
dwindling to a sound like stifled sobs.
The sky brightened, I climbed back toward the path.
Alone, the old man made farewells.

Grief Again
(Four quatrains from a group of twelve)

I

All these petty statelets: still at lance and steed.
What's my old garden like today?
Last visit, there were few I knew.
Now, there are more new battlefields
                     than old friends left.

II

Here I remain, a petty officer in exile
while the family needs me home to farm.
But the year grows late,
wild grasses, tall along the paths.
I'm afraid I'd miss my own rude gate.

III

Arrows, chased with gold!
Black oxtails on their banner poles.
Since this dusty wind first rose . . .
it's been hard to travel.

IV

Barbarians. How can there be so many?
Shield and spear: unwilling to put by.
At the village gate, listen to the children
laugh and shout; play war.

Passing the Ferry

Mount Heng's hard by.
The River Hsiang flows east from here.
Mild breezes draw the oarsman on,
and spring sun rises midst the mountain clouds.
I turn my head as we pass the ferry;
still, along the banks, many fine groves of maple.
Silver minnows struggle in the fine mesh nets;
Yellow birds proclaim, above, in joyous notes:
if even these tiny things know freedom from bondage,
ought not compassion be the very heart of man?
The jug remains; there is still wine.
My lute lies silent on my knees.
Sages, Worthies, too, lie still and mute, small lonely men.
I rest my eyes, and loosen my robes to the breeze.

On Seeing the Sword Dance Performed by a Disciple of Madam Kung-sun

Long ago there was a beauty, Kung-sun her name.
In a single gesture of her sword dance all the world was
        overthrown.
And Heaven and Earth bowed long before her.
Bending back, the bow of Great I's shot, and nine suns falling.
Rising up, a heavenly being, aloft, on dragons soaring.
Approaching: she is lightning, thunder; holds the harvest of
        storm's fury.
Staying: rivers and oceans, congealed, as clear light.
Deep red lips and pearl-sewn sleeves are quiet,
late now, from one disciple only does such fragrance come.
The lady of Lin-ying at White Emperor Town,
the fair dance to the old song, and the spirits soaring.
And when I asked and found whence came such art,
I pondered time, and change, and grew still sadder.
Ming-huang's waiting maids; eight thousand,
and Madam Kun-sun's sword dance stood premier.
Now fifty years, a single simple gesture of the palm,
dust in the wind, quicksilver, dusk, our Royal House.
The Pear Garden's pupils, like the mist they all are scattered;
this lady's fading beauty brightens the cold sun.
South of Gold Grain Hill, the trees: grown to full
        hand's span.
Here in Chü-t'ang Gorge, the grasses wither.
The feasts, the pipes; songs end again.
The utmost joy, then sadness comes; moon rises, east.
The old man can't know where he's to go,
feet sore, wild hills, turning, deep in sorrow.

Meeting Li Kuei-nien South of the River

At the prince of Ch'i's house, we met often.
At Ts'ui's so many times, so many years,
I heard you sing.
Now . . .
          How beautiful it is, here
             South of the River
flowers fall. We meet again.

Thoughts While Traveling by Night

Slender grass, light breeze on the banks.
Tall mast, a solitary night on board.
A star falls, and the vast plain seems broader.
Surging moon, on the Great River flows.
Can fame grow from *wen* alone?
This servant of the people, now old and sick, must let that be.
Afloat, afloat, just so . . .
Heaven, and Earth, and one black gull.

Ch'ien Ch'i (722–780?)

Gazing from High on the Mountain on the Rainy Sea and Thinking of the Monks in the Yu-lin Monastery

From the mountain, rain upon the sea,
and dripping foam from the misty trees.
It looks as if, in that vastness,
those dark isles might any moment fly away.

Nature has angered the eight-headed spirit-serpent of the sea.
The rushing tides stir up the road of the clouds.
The true men ever fill my thoughts,
but a single reed can't float across.
Sad thought of the times at Red Cliff
wishing I could harness the wild swans, and drive.

The Master of Hsiang Plays His Lute

So well he plays his cloud-topped lute,
we hear the Lady of the River.
The god of the stream is moved to dance in emptiness.
The traveler of Ch'u can't bear to listen.
A bitter tune, to chill both gold and stone.
Pure notes pierce gloomy dark.
Deep green *wu-t'ung* brings sad thoughts on.
White iris there recalls a certain fragrance.
The waters flow, between Hsiang's banks.
Mournful winds cross Lake Tung-t'ing.
Song done, and no one to be seen.
On the river, many peaks, all green.

Wei Ying-wu (736–830)

The West River at Ch'u-chou

Alone, for love of hidden herbs, which flourish by the stream.
Above, the yellow oriole sings deep among the trees.
Spring's flood tides, and rain, together, to this evening come.
No man at the ferry: boat drifts there, on its own.

On Mount Lang-ya

At Stone Gate there is snow, no trace of travel.
Pine Valley's mists, so full of fragrances.
To the crumbs of our meal in the court, cold birds come down.
A tattered robe hangs on the tree; the old monk's dead.

Li I (748–827)

Northern Campaign

After T'ien-shan's snows, cold desert wind.
Flute sounds all about, the going hard.
Three hundred thousand men, among these rocks,
this once, as one, together turn: gaze on the moon.

Song of the South of the River

Married to a Chü-t'ang river trader.
Morn, and morn, and tidings never come.
If I had only known how faithful tide can be . . .
Better to have wed a player
on the waves of the tidal bore.

Chang Chi (768–830)

Coming at Night to a Fisherman's Hut

Fisherman's hut, by the mouth of the river,
the water of the lake to his brushwood gate.
The traveler would beg night's lodging,
but the master's not yet home.
The bamboo's thick, the village far.
Moon rises. Fishing boats are few.
There! Far off, along the sandy shore,
the spring breeze moving in his cloak of straw!

Moored at Maple Bridge

Moon sets, crow caws, frost fills the heavens.
River maples, fisherman's fires, my eyes
face all this sadness.
Han Shan's temple: here outside the walls of Gusu.
Middle of the night, bell's tone, like a stone struck,
visits every traveler's boat.

Wang Chien (768–833)

The New Wife

On the third day she went down to the kitchen,
washed her hands, prepared the broth.
Still unaware of her new mother's likings,
she asked his sister to taste.

Liu Yu-hsi (772–842)

The City of Stones

Wrapped safe, it seemed, this ancient land, in mountains.
Now tides rise against the empty wall, ebb quietly.
East of the River Huai, same moon as of those days,
night grows again, upon the battlements.

Song of the Bamboo Stalks

Red blossoms: mountain peach, upon the heights.
Shu River: floods of spring caress the mountain, flowing.
The flowers bloom and fade, so like his love.
The waters run on endlessly: my sorrow.

Po Chu-i (772–846)

Grass on the Ancient Plain

So tender, so tender, the grasses on the plain,
in one year, to wither, then flourish.
Wildfire cannot burn them away.
Spring breezes' breath, they spring again,
their distant fragrance on the ancient way,
their sunlit emerald greens the ruined walls.
Seeing you off again, dear friend,
sighing, sighing, full of parting's pain.

The Charcoal Man

The old charcoal man
cuts wood and seasons coals up on South Mountain.
Face full of ashes, the color of smoke,
hair white at the temples, ten fingers black,
sells charcoal, gets money, and where does it go?
For the clothes on his body and the food that he eats.
Yet sadly though those clothes are thin,
he's so worried for the price of charcoal
that he prays the weather cold.
Last night, on the city wall, a foot of snow.
Dawn, he loads his cart, tracks over ice.
The ox tired, the man hungry, the sun already high,
south of the market, outside the gate, in the mud, they rest.
So elegant these prancing horsemen, who are they?
Yellow-robed official, with his white-robed boy.
Hand holds a written order, mouth spouts "The Emperor."
They turn the cart. They curse the ox. Head north.
A thousand pounds of charcoal in that cart . . .
And if they commandeer, can he complain?
Half a piece of scarlet gauze, three yards of silk:
tied round the ox's head, this charcoal's price.

Liu Tsung-yuan (773–819)

The Old Fisherman

The old fisherman spends his night beneath the western cliffs.
At dawn, he boils Hsiang's waters, burns bamboo of Ch'u.

When the mist's burned off, and the sun's come out, he's gone.
The slap of the oars: the mountain waters green.
Turn and look, at heaven's edge, he's moving with the flow.
Above the cliffs, the aimless clouds go too.

River Snow

A thousand mountains, no birds fly.
Ten thousand paths, no footprints.
Lone skiff, rush-cloaked old man.
Fishing alone, cold river snow.

Chia Tao (779–843)

Searching, and Not Finding, the Hermit

Beneath the pines I asked the boy.
"The master's gone in search of simples . . .
He's on the mountain over there:
clouds so thick, I can't tell where."

Passing the Night in a Village Inn

This bed's pillow's a stone in the stream
that runs from the wellspring to the bamboo's pool.
The traveler has not slept, as midnight goes.
Alone, he listens: the mountain rain arrives.

Li Ho (790–816)

Don't Go Out, Sir!

Heaven's dark,
the earth shut tight.
The nine-headed serpent feeds on our souls.
Snow and frost snap our bones.
The dogs, set loose, snarl to our scent,
licking their paws at the thought of the flesh
of men who go girdled in orchids.
When the emperor sends his chariot to bear you away,
then all your hardships will end.
Jade stars dot your sword, of yellow gold will be your yoke.
But though I go horseback, there is no way home.
The waves that drowned Li-yang stand tall as a mountain.
Venomous dragons glare at me, rattling their rings of gold,
and lions and griffins, slavering, drool.
Pao Chiao, a whole lifetime, slept on straw.
Yen Hui's hair, at twenty-nine, was mottled white.
Yen Hui's blood was not corrupted.
Nor had Pao offended Heaven.
Heaven feared those jaws would close,
therefore advanced them so . . .
Clear as it is, if you still doubt,
think on the madman who raved by the wall.

The Tomb of Su Hsiao-hsiao

On the solitary orchid, dew:
like tear-filled eyes.

Nothing to tie our hearts together.
Misty blossoms, I cannot bear to cut.
Grass for her carpet;
pines, her roof.
The wind her robe and
water sounds her pendants.
There, painted carriages
are waiting in the night,
green candles cool,
weary with brilliance.
Beneath the Western Mound,
wind drives the rain.

Tu Mu (803–852)

Confession

Soul sunk in Chiang-nan, wandering with wine.
All beauties' hearts are broken, if they fall into my hands.
Ten years dozing, Yang-chou dreams . . .
I have won a name among these pleasure houses:
they call me "the heartless man."

Poem of Parting

Great love could seem indifference.
The only hint before the cup: we cannot smile.
Only the candle's not heartless:
wept tears for us until the dawn.

Spring South of the River

Song of the oriole, a thousand *li*, reds brighten on the green.
Streamside village, mountains for walls, wind in the tavern banner.
Here, four hundred eighty temples, in the southern dynasties . . .
Now how many towers, terraces? The misting rain.

Traveling among Mountains

Far climbing Cold Mountain, rocky path turns.
There, where clouds grow, some man's home.
I halt the carriage, sit adoring, evening, maple grove;
these frosted leaves: far redder than March bloom.

Coming Home

The children pull at my coat and inquire,
"You've come home, oh, why so late?
Who were you fighting with all these years,
to win that head of white hair?"

Li Shang-yin (813–858)

Untitled

Meeting is hard; parting, hard too.
The east wind's feeble, yet the hundred flowers fall.
Spring silkworm spins its silk until it dies.

The candle sheds its tears till wick is ashes.
The morning mirror grieves. Clouds of hair are changing.
Song of the night, know moonlight's cold.
From here to Mount P'eng the way's not long
but the Green Bird is attentive, watches close.

Untitled

Phoenix tails, the fragrant silk, how many gauzy folds,
green filigrees, the canopy, late into night she sews.
The fan cuts the moon's light, it cannot hide her blush.
The carriage goes, the thunder sounds, words can't get through.
Long in silent solitude, as candle burns to dark.
Cut off, no word, and who would bring red pomegranate wine?
The piebald horse is tied as always to the trailing willow tree
but where is the southwest wind, where the good breeze?

Wang Chia (9th century)

Day of the Spring Sacrifice

Lake of the Geese at the foot of the mountain, rice and millet fat.
Henhouse and pigpen shut up tight.
Shadows of the mulberries grow long, the spring-fest ended.
Propped each on each, the drunken, wandering home.

Ch'en T'ao (9th century)

Song of Lung-hsi

Sworn to the death to exterminate the Huns:
five thousand sable doublets on that alien ground.
Pity, by Lost River there, those bones,
men still, in the dreams of their lovers.

Tu Hsun-ho (846–904)

See a Friend Off to Wu

I see you to Ku-su.
Homes there, sleeping by the stream.
Ancient palace, few abandoned spots.
And by the harbor, many little bridges.
In the night market, lotus, fruit and roots.
On the spring barges, satins and gauze.
Know, far off, the moon still watches.
Think of me there, in the fisherman's song.

Li P'in (9th century)

Fording the Han River

Crags cut sound. No word past
winter's gone. I come
with spring, and the closer
I come, the more afraid.
Don't dare to ask
word of you.

Out of Place and Time: Six Zen Master Poets of the T'ang

IN THE T'ANG, SOUTHERN SCHOOL CH'AN (ZEN) BUDDHISM was adopted by perhaps the majority of traditional poets as the favored route to spiritual enlightenment. Even so, Zen poetry by monk practitioners remained something of a separate (and sometimes more than equal) poetic art, and thus I have decided to place the poems of the six most important monk-poets of the Golden Age in a special place, outside chronological order, or, as the Zen meditator is, outside of time.

Actually, the first three of the monk-poets weren't even necessarily really monks. All three are essentially legendary figures. One, Wang Fan-chih, was the creation of Buddhist schoolteachers. He spouted pious doggerel for little kids' primers. Another, of the same name, who like the first flourished in the the eighth century, was an urban wild man, what one would probably call a bohemian today. Their work was extremely popular in T'ang and Sung but then was totally lost, only to be rediscovered conflated, in the twentieth century in the famous temple library of T'un-huang, among materials sealed up around 1135 as the borders of the Chinese empire shrank. Only the latter's work appears here.

The legendary Han Shan has been popular in China and Japan since the first appearance of his poems, also in the eighth century. Their reappearance in the translations of the great American Beat generation poet Gary Snyder helped, as much as Snyder's often Zen-inspired poetry itself, to work a positive change in American culture. Translations of the poems of Han Shan's legendary sidekick Shih Te, "the Foundling," have appeared since Snyder's translations of Han Shan.

Of the other three historical monk-poets, Chiao Jan (730–799) was a T'ang aristocrat turned monk who was witness in his youth to the greatest period of the Golden Age. His poetry is highly civilized and urbane, yet has a witty, even biting edge; it clearly owes much to the influence of the "wild men."

The poetry in this section by Chia Tao (779–843), is presented here by his monk name, Wu Pen. He first witnessed the cataclysmic decline of the empire as a monk. Later, pulled I think by his bodhisattva oath (to strive to liberate all beings from suffering) rather than any vulgar desire for worldly success or fame, he served as a minor government official under the patronage of the nominally anti-Buddhist poet official Han Yu. The last poet in the group, Kuan Hsiu (832–912), became a monk at an early age, probably to avoid starvation. In his own lifetime he was regarded as the greatest poet of his age. His vigorously creative use of the vernacular influenced the greatest of the Sung poets, as did his courageous and aggressive social protest poetry (see, for instance, "Bad Government," p. 142. In addition he was a serious political thinker, among the first to propose a synthesis of Confucianism, Taoism, and Buddhism as a new ruling ideology. This was a pretty revolutionary idea. Sung thinkers took two centuries to fully embrace it. Also a portrait painter, Kuan Hsiu developed an individualistic style that made him an important figure in the history of Chinese graphic art as well. Sometimes a genius finds his time, and sometimes he doesn't.

It may not be out of place to mention here that from the Sung dynasty on, Zen monasteries were centers of traditional culture. The brilliant and charismatic half-blind orphan dwarf who became the first emperor of the Ming was educated in a Buddhist monastery. In the Ming and Ch'ing, the last two traditional dynasties, a really significant proportion of the best traditional poetry was created by monks like Han-shan Te-ch'ing (also the last great commentator on Lao Tzu's Taoist classic *Tao Te Ching*) and Ching-an, a monk and abbot who lived into the twentieth century.

Wang Fan-chih (8th century)

I

A long time ago, before I was born
it was dark. There was nothing, I knew.
The Lord of Heaven made life for me,
but what did he give me life for?
Without clothes, I knew cold,
without food, I knew hunger.
Get back to the Lord of Heaven for me . . .
ask him could he please
get me back to before I was born.

II

When I saw him die,
my guts were on fire:
not that I pitied *him*,
just that it might be my turn next.

III

Others go astride great chargers;
me, on my ass.
Then there's the guy under a load of firewood.
I compare me to both.

IV

Nobody lives to be a hundred.
But they try to write rhymes that'll last a thousand.
Forge an iron gate to fence out the demons:
demons watch, clapping, and laughing.

V

Wang Fan-chih wears his socks inside out,
everybody knows that's all wrong.
But he'd rather poke you in the eye
than keep his feet in the dark.

VI

Having power need not warp your heart and mind,
but if you cheat folks, you put yourself in danger.
Just look at the fire on the wood:
once it's burned up the fuel, the *fire's* gone too.

Han Shan (8th century)

I

Human beings live in the dirt,
like bugs in a filthy bowl.
All day long crawling around and around,

never getting over the edge.
Even spiritual masters can't make it,
racking their brains for schemes and plans.
The months and the years, a running river:
then there's the day you wake up old.

II

Parrots fly free in the western lands.
Forest huntsmen net them, bring them here.
Courtesans love to play with them, and so
they're well known at court, in and out all day.

They're given golden cages to dwell in,
but bolted in, their robes of plumes are ruined.
Better a swan, or a crane . . .
riding the winds high up, well known
to the clouds where they fly.

III

Mr. Wang's *degree* says Flourishing Talent.
He loves to find fault with my poems.
He says I don't follow the "regulations,"
and don't use the "right" techniques.
He says I don't use the four tones correctly,
and just stick in words any which way.
I laugh at what *he* calls poetry: a blind man's
rhymes: lukewarm praise of the sun.

IV

Trying to talk light into dark mysteries:
all moon bright night,
searching reason, sun coming on to dawn.
Ten thousand schemes, just muddy tracks.
True magic, just to see the *true self* come:
true self, and the *thus come* Buddha, One.

V

The gorge is long, rocks, and rocks and rocks, jut up,
the torrent's wide, reeds almost hide the other side.
The moss is slippery even without rain.
The pines sing: the wind is real enough.
Who's ready to leap free of the world's traces:
come sit with me among white clouds?

VI

My old landlady
got rich three or four years ago.
Used to be poorer than me,
now she laughs that I don't have money.
She laughs that I've fallen behind.
I laugh that she's gotten ahead.
Both of us laughing, no stopping us.
Landlady, and Lord of the West.

VII

How many T'ien T'ai mountain monks,
don't really know what's up,
and just talk idle nonsense?

Shih Te (8th century)

I

You say, "If you want to be happy,
there's no way but to be a hermit.
Flowers in the grove are better than brocade.
Every single season's colors new.
Just sit by a cliff and turn your head
to watch the moon's ball roll."
And me? I ought to be at joyous ease,
but I can't help thinking of the people in the world.

II

When I was young I studied books, and swordsmanship,
and rode off with a shout to the capital,
where I heard the barbarians had been driven off already . . .
there was no place left for heroes.
So I came back to these crested peaks,
lay down and listened to the clear stream's flow.
Young men dream of glory:
monkeys riding on the ox's back.

III

I've always been Shih Te, the Foundling.
It's not some accidental title.
Yet I'm not without a family.
Han Shan is my brother.
Two men with hearts a lot alike.
No need for vulgar love.
If you want to know how old we are . . .
like the Yellow River, that's unclear.

IV

You want to learn to catch a mouse?
Don't try to learn from a pampered cat.
If you want to learn the nature of the world,
don't study fine bound books.
The True Jewel's in a coarse bag.
The Buddha nature stops at huts.
The whole herd of folks who clutch at appearances
never seem to make the connection.

V

My poems are poems;
some people call them sermons.
Well now, poems and sermons share one thing;
when you read them you got to be careful.
Keep at it. Get into detail.
Don't just claim they're easy.

If you were to live your life like that,
a lot of funny things might happen.

Chiao Jan (730–799)

Inscribed on the Wall of the Hut by the Lake

If you want to be a mountain dweller . . .
no need to trek to India to find a mountain . . .
I've got a thousand peaks
to pick from, right here in this lake.
Fragrant grasses, white clouds,
to hold me here.
What holds you there,
world-dweller?

To Be Shown to the Monks at a Certain Temple

Not yet to the shore of nondoing,
it's silly to be sad you're not moored yet . . .
Eastmount's white clouds say
to keep on moving, even
if it's evening, even if it's fall.

At Gusu

The ancient terrace now invisible:
autumn grasses wither, there

where once the king of Wu stood
proud and strong. A thousand
years of moonlight on the grass:
how often did he gaze upon it?
Now the moon will rise again,
but he will not. A world of men have
gazed, will gaze, upon great
Gusu Mountain. Here dwells a placid spirit.
Deer herd to blur men's footprints.
Here too Hsi-tzu's fair simplicity, seductive
lips brought an empire crashing down:
now, *that all is change is clear:*
at Cold Peak, a little heap of dirt.

Metaphor

My Tao: at the root, there's no me . . .
yet I don't despise worldly men.
Just now I've been into the city . . .
so I know I really mean that.

Good-byes

I've heard that even "men of feeling"
don't treasure the feeling of parting.
Frosty sky drips a chill
on the cold city wall.
The long night spreads
like water overflowing.
There's the sound of the watch-horn, too.

The Zen man's heart is empty, yes,
of all but these.

Sending Off a Friend amid the Cries of Gibbons

You'll go ten thousand miles
beyond those western mountains . . .
Three gibbons' cries,
a chasm full of moonlight . . .
How long's this road been here?
How many travelers
have wet their sleeves beside it?
A broken wall divides the drooping shadows.
Rushing rapids sing a bitter song.
In the cold, when we have finally parted,
it will be all the more wounding to hear.

Gazing at the Moon from South Tower

Moon tonight, and everyone's moon-gazing,
but I'm alone, and in love with this tower.
Threads of cloud are shattered in the stream:
trailing willow is the picture of late fall.
As it brightens, you can see a thousand peaks.
Far off, the veins of ridges flow.
Mountain passes . . .
will I ever climb again?
I stand alone,
and let the border sadness rise.

Wu Pen (Chia Tao, 779–843)

After Finishing a Poem

Those two lines cost me three years:
I chant them once and get two more, of tears.
Friend, if you don't like them . . .
I'll go home, and lie down,
in the ancient mountain autumn.

Overnight at a Mountain Temple

Flock of peaks hunched up
and colored cold. The path forks
here, toward the temple.
A falling star flares behind bare trees,
and the moon breasts the current of the clouds.
Few men come to the very top . . .
One tall pine won't hold a flock of cranes.
One monk here, at eighty,
has never heard tell
of the "world" down below.

Quatrain

At the bottom of the ocean: the moon,
bright moon, round as the wheel of the sky.
Just get a single hand full of this glory . . .
And you could buy a thousand miles of spring.

A Letter Sent

The family's living up Brocade Creek,
while I've struggled off to this distant sea.
Of ten letters sent, maybe one gets through,
and when it does, it says
another year's gone by.

The Swordsman

Ten long years I've honed this sword:
frost white blade as yet untried.
Today, like any other gentleman,
it's looking for injustice.

Extempore

Midnight, heart startled, I rise,
to take the path to Long Cascade:
the trees of the grove are swallowed in white dew:
a dipper of stars, in the clear dark sky.

Kuan Hsiu (832–912)

Letter to the Wild Monk

Other than the birds, who loves you?
Lordly peaks, your neighbors.

White head cold pillowed on a stone.
Gray robe ragged but not soiled.
Chestnuts pile up on your path.
Monkeys circle where you sit.
If you ever set up another zendo,
I swear I'll be the one who sweeps the floors.

Moored on Fall River

Banks like Lake Tung-t'ing, but the hills too steep.
Boat floats the clear stream, but the cold climbs in my berth.
White moon rides a high wind, and I can't sleep.
Among the withered reeds, the fisherman's a nightmare.

Spending the Night in a Little Village

Hard traveling, and then a little village, for the night:
a year of plenty, chickens, dogs, it's raucous as a market town.
Come out to meet the stranger in the dusk:
whole families, laughing, happy:
beneath the moon, seining up fish from the pool.

To an Old Monk on Mount T'ien T'ai

Living alone where none other dwells,
shrine among the pines where mountain tints encroach,
this old man's been ninety years a monk:
heart beyond the clouds a lifetime long.
White hair hangs down, *his* head's unshaven:

clear black pupils smile deep mysteries.
He can still point to the orphan moon
for me alone, relaxing his discipline, this moment.

Thinking of the Old Mountains toward the End of Autumn

Used to live north of Square Hut . . .
Nobody knew my name.
Up through the clouds to harvest my grain,
climbing like an ant into the tree to pick the oranges.
Saw a tiger wander by that lonesome village . . .
Anyone could grow white-haired
living a life like that.

Song of the Palace of Ch'en

Think sad thoughts of other days,
those palace gates, overflowing . . .
Reckless feasting, feckless loves: no Sages, there.
Jade trees' blossoms singing, there,
among a hundred flowers.
Coral jeweled, the very window frames,
sun from the sea, scattered jewels.
Great ministers to audience; Mi' Lord
still in his cups, and even when he'd sobered
few wise words got past *his* ears.
So. The Palace of Ch'en
is rubble in this farmer's field,
and the peasant's plow turns up the shards
of a courtier's mirror.

Bad Government

Sleet and rain, as if the pot were boiling.
Winds whack like the crack of an axe.
An old man, an old old man,
toward sunset crept into my hut.
He sighed, sighed he, as if to himself,
"These rulers, so cruel: why, tell me
why they must steal till we starve,
and then slice off the skin from our bones?
For a song from some beauty
they'll go back on sworn words;
for a song from some tart,
they'll tear our huts down . . .
for a song, for a sweet song or two,
they'll slaughter ten thousand like me, or
like you. You can cry as you will, let
your hair turn pure white,
let your whole clan go hungry . . .
no good wind will blow
no gentle breeze
begin again.
Lord Locust Plague, and Baron Bandit Bug,
one east, one west, one north, one south,
We're surrounded."

On the Border: Three Poems

I

Mountains: no green
and no clean water.

poisonous wind, and
sands rank with blood stench.
Tartars on horseback
hate the birds, flying:
draw bows at will, to bring them down.
you can hear their cries
from above the clouds.

II

Gusts blow a cloud up, sudden
from the sand: we can tell the
Tartars are massing to cross the River Liao.
Gulping the dust of fear, here, now, us
border guards: sure we're ghosts, already.

III

In Green Mound Cave, they say
a white wolf dwells.
Once in a while it comes out
looks east, and howls
and howls
and howls.
Paint that for me, if you can,
my painter friend.

Song of the Righteous Man

Born before me, born
before, I'll never meet him.

He loved peace, but there was no peace,
so he set his brows like bolts of stars . . .

Yellow dusk, then rain and sleet
and sky like a bruise, like a cancer.

He's gone, now, and
I'll not know where.

Leaving It to You

Self-evident, truth mistakes no thing.
But my heart's a long way from there
and no thing's clear to me.
Yellow gold is almost all burned up
by my desire:
white hair grows beside the fire.
Bitter indecision, choose This, or maybe That:
even spirit speaks in riddles,
and it makes it hard to harvest
the essence of a single day.
Catch the wind, while you tether the shadows.
Faith, or a man who'll stand by his word, is all
there is, there is no disputing.

Written in the Mountains

A mountain's a palace
for all things crystalline and pure:
there's not a speck of dust
on a single one of all these flowers.

When we start chanting poems like madmen
it sets all the peaks to dancing.
And once we've put the brush to work
even the sky becomes mere ornament.
For you and me the joy's in the doing
and I'm damned if I care about "talent."

But if, my friend, from time to time
you hear sounds like ghostly laughter . . .
It's all the great mad poets, dead,
and just dropping in for a listen.

Late Autumn, Sent to a Gentleman at Wu-ch'ang

Heard you're at War-Bright Town, living by the river:
cypress withers, even locust rots, in these wartime winds.
I know you're addicted to poetry still:
the drug you crave is hard to come by in a place like that.
So I send this: frost sparkle and reed flowers,
in a tincture of bright moonlight.

PART FOUR

A Few Strong Voices Still Singing

Poetry from the Sung (960–1279), Yuan (1279–1368),
Ming (1368–1628), and Ch'ing (1644–1911)
Dynasties to the Twentieth Century

Introduction to Poetry from the Sung, Yuan, Ming, and Ch'ing Dynasties to the Twentieth Century

WHAT WE CALL "HISTORY" HAS PRETTY MUCH EVERYWHERE always been punctuated by soldiers marching to a halt where kings, emperors, or presidents-for-life pronounce a glorious and perhaps perpetual peace. So the Sung also began, in 960, after a hundred years of flailing failure by the T'ang and a chaotic interregnum of another fifty-some years of war.

In China, *wen* was in traditional culture valued above *wu*. Wen, which included poetry among its necessary communications skills, also included moral and ethical courage, the sometimes death-defying willingness to stand up to temporal authority in support of the timeless ultimate authority of the people, embodied in the wisdom of the "Sages" of Confucianism, Taoism, and Buddhism. Wu certainly had its attractions, as we have seen in the earliest Chinese poetry. There is no denying the appeal of physical courage, the willingness to follow orders without questioning, even to the death (at least in a good cause, or for one's brothers in arms). We also recognize the appeal of the mostly oral communication skills that create the charisma of a warrior captain, in European culture from Homer and from Shakespeare among many other poets.

But, maybe just because of the primacy of *wen* as a cultural value in China, warfare itself, as a glorious enterprise, doesn't produce much poetry. The effects of War on the civilian population certainly do, as we have seen in the work of Tu Fu, among others. The last of the great T'ang poets, the Zen monk Kuan Hsiu, perhaps came closest to dealing directly with war, though he did not glorify it, as he satirized warlords and wrote of the travails of border guards. But when, at last, true peace did come, poets felt released, at last, to write "silly love songs" if they pleased.

The end of the great age of classical Chinese poetry begins in the Sung. But, of course, there were many more fine poets, even some great ones, who lived and wrote throughout the period from the end of the T'ang through the beginning of the twentieth century. It was a thousand years before the end of the writing of classical poetry. If all that was left of the grand tradition in 960 was the gold of embers in the hearth, there was plenty of warmth in the fireplace, and a single breath of poetic genius in the room of each remaining dynasty (Sung, Yuan, Ming, and Ch'ing) was still able bring up a real flame. It's also true that in each of those dynasties, there were more than enough great poets and great poems to fill a library, much less a little book like this, so that there will be no falling off in quality here.

Mei Yao-ch'en (1002–1060), Liu Yung (fl. 1034), and Ou-yang Hsiu (1007–1072), the next poets in the anthology, would all unquestionably be poets of the first rank in any period in Chinese history. Su Shih (1037–1101), also known as Su Tung-p'o, has no more than four or five peers in the whole proud tradition. Li Ch'ing-chao (1084–c. 1151) is among those peers and is also, without any doubt, the best of a sadly short list of accomplished female poets.

Traditional literary historians have acknowledged Sung as the period of the fullest flowering of the *tz'u* form. That means that now poets wrote *tz'u* poems in addition to the many kinds of *shih*. As I mentioned in the introduction, *t'zu* are poems written to match the wording of preexisting songs (the verb for "writing" a *tz'u* means literally to "fill in," to drop words in the slots provided by a song pattern). *Tz'u* actually became popular toward the end of the T'ang. But in the early Sung, Liu Yung's convincingly romantic love songs became extraordinarily popular. Ou-yang Hsiu was in his youth a precociously talented young official who teetered on the edge of banishment for unconventional behavior, including well-publicized liaisons with famous courtesans. In maturity he was a literary polymath, a powerful official, and a generous patron of other truly talented poets and officials. When he deigned to put his hand to the writing of *tz'u*, a stellar batch of others, including Su Shih, followed, if not beginning to write in the form, at least beginning to admit to it. All of Li Ch'ing-chao's poems are in the form, and without the validation of a literary kingmaker like Ou-yang, all her work, and the *tz'u* itself, might never have been recognized as "authentic" poetic art.

But the essence of the *tz'u* was freedom. In the beginning, young writers, outsiders, wrote *tz'u* in imitation of "barbarian" songs or courtesans' songs, daring to be inspired by the romance of those lives and the new rhythms of their music. So the form very quickly lost its liveliness when court poets joined in. They tended to favor the application of strict phonetic and grammatical regulation, à la the "regulated verse" of the T'ang.

For the most part, in this final section, for both the *tz'u* and its Yuan dynasty reincarnations, the various kinds of *ch'u* poems (with only a few exceptions), I have followed Western convention, titling otherwise untitled *tz'u* poems with a full or abbreviated first line rather than, as is the Chinese convention, titling them with the title of the tune that dictated their line lengths in Chinese. Indeed, with some of the flimsier (but not unpleasing) Yuan *san-ch'u*, I've left off titles entirely.

The Yuan dynasty is a period that includes three beginning dates: 1226, when the Mongols conquered north China; 1260, when they are credited with finally occupying the rest of China; and 1280, when "pacification" was complete enough to allow the famous Kublai Khan to actually claim the throne of China. By 1368, less than a century after they declared the conquest triumphantly completed, the last of the Mongol ruling classes had run home to the Gobi, while the vast majority of ordinary Mongol folks, lately warrior conquerors but having grown to prefer life as common folk in civilized China to life as ordinary folk in tents in the Gobi, had adopted Chinese surnames and blended happily into the populace of the new Ming dynasty.

The Yuan probably didn't produce a single *great poet*, though the dramatist Kuan Han-ch'ing, Ma Chih-yuan, Po P'u, and Chang Yang-hao are all worthy of consideration. But, maybe because of the almost complete social disorder of the period, there is a spirit in Yuan poetry that may always have existed in China but was certainly seldom seen. There are wits and ironists. Consider carefully whether a Yuan poet is bragging or complaining when he says he's drunk or when she says she's reached "enlightenment."

A new cultural "invention," the operatic drama—actually a theatrical performance mixing fancy verse with straight vernacular prose dialogue, a little more like what we call Shakespearean theater than like present-day Chinese opera—achieved a flourishing commercial popularity and increasing artistic sophistication. Most of the poets presented in this section, most certainly including the wildly bohemian Kuan Han-ch'ing, made their names in the creation of theatrical pieces for commercial performance, thereby becoming among the first Chinese *professional* men of letters, the first of the traditionally educated literati to actually make a living directly from their literary work.

The new *san-ch'u* form, similar to the *tz'u* but freer in execution and including both short lyrics and more complex longer forms suited to narrative and/or dramatic or operatic creation, was wildly popular.

Both blatant hedonistic escapism and the search for personal salvation through Buddhist or Taoist enlightenment are themes more often chosen than in earlier dynasties. These themes may seem particularly appropriate to a period such as the Yuan, and it is also interesting to see how easily the refugee and the socially displaced view their lives and their sufferings, as represented in poetry, as somehow easier to bear when they are literarily refigured by connection with the great Ch'u Yuan, his "Fisherman," or the Seven Sages of the Bamboo Grove. Again and again in Yuan poems, you will notice T'ao Ch'ien and of course Li Po playing a similar role. Just to get drunk, or just to sit in meditation is one thing (or two); to sit with heroes from other times who share your existential pain seems to be another.

The Ming dynasty was no doubt an "interesting time." Its founder was a true genius, but one who quickly fell under the spell of absolute power, creating a thoroughly evil government to protect his perhaps beautifully utopian dream. Nonetheless it was also in this dynasty that Chinese explorers reached the Cape of Good Hope a full sixty years before the Portuguese pirate-colonialists who were coming slowly down the west coast of Africa. The great ships built in China for the trip in the fourteenth century were unrivaled in the world in size and seaworthiness until the nineteenth century, but the Chinese sailors, merchants, and intelligence officers aboard those great ships, having reached southern Africa without finding anything worth trading for or any naval or political power that looked at all threatening, returned to China.

Though the Ming has been famous in the West for its insularity, it was a lively, creative society. It is renowned for its landscape painting in a variety of styles and for its vibrantly beautiful ceramics. Among the Chinese it is remarked for the creation of a vibrant and forceful, Zen-influenced *neo*-neo-Confucianism, developed by Wang Yang-ming (1472–1579). Wang was extraordinarily successful as a troubleshooting imperial official, and his practical successes helped his democratic philosophy attract a following that continued to grow in spite of official suppression. The Ming also saw a creative revival of Zen Buddhism itself, one that left its mark on popular prose fiction, as well as on classical poetry and painting, in both the Ming and the final dynasty, the Ch'ing. The great novel *Hsi Yu Chi*, offered in an expertly condensed English translation as *Monkey* by the master translator of Asian literature

Arthur Waley, is both a delightfully humorous picaresque novel and a successful allegorical treatment of themes common to both Zen and Wang Yang-ming's Confucian thought.

But for all my efforts to assure you of its vitality, as you might have already guessed, the Ming was not a great period for poetry. No Ming poet appears in Robert Payne's *The White Pony*, the best-selling English-language anthology of Chinese poetry of the twentieth century, and very little is to be found in its closest competitor, the much larger and still popular Doubleday anthology *Sunflower Splendor*. But the best of Ming poetry reflects the thought of the times. It is lively, humorous, and intellectually challenging. The poets I've chosen to represent the Ming include a Confucian martyr, a madman, a monk (maybe the greatest Zen monk-poet and scholar-commentator of any dynasty), and four extremely talented and, as usual, nearly anonymous women. We know these women's names but, so far as I can tell, nothing more about them than these beautiful little poems. I suspect all were what used to be known as ladies of the evening. As poets they are simply *heroines*.

Kao Ch'i (1336–1374), whom I earlier referred to as a martyr, was likely the best male poet of the Ming. His complete works might well have been more impressive if he hadn't been beheaded, on flimsy charges, at the age of thirty-eight. The Ming was a good period to choose the anonymity of the professional fiction writer, for more reasons than one. The madman is Hsu Wei (1521–1593). The brilliant and strange quatrains of this extremely brilliant and very strange painter, poet, dramatist, wife murderer (he actually served seven years in prison), and apparently sometimes effective officer of state were translated by my friend Jim Cryer under a grant from the National Endowment for the Arts.

Aside from Hui Neng and his five main disciples in eighth-century (T'ang) China, Han-shan Te-ch'ing (1546–1623) is without doubt the most influential Zen monk in the history of the transmission of Zen (Ch'an) Buddhism. As abbot of a famous monastery, he was a player in Ming politics, and though he lacks a beheading to prove his commitment, he did spend time in prison and in exile. It seems ridiculous to expect such a man in such a time to be a poet at all, much less a great one, but he was. Part of the possible paradox is explained by the fact that he clearly had a wonderful self-effacing sense of humor: the "Han Shan" in his name is definitely meant to *refer* to the madman poet-bodhisattva Han Shan of the T'ang, but the *character* used to produce the Han syllable in pronouncing the name includes the word for "to dare" above the word for "heart-and-mind" followed by the word *moun-tain*, the same character that makes the Shan in Han Shan's name. Han-shan Te-ch'ing borrows the glory of his already vastly famous predecessor and adds a daring heart, but as it turns out the character I just described *means* "silly" or even "stupid." Making his self-applied name all the sillier is the fact that Te-ch'ing literally means "virtuous prince," giving us Stupid Mountain Virtuous Prince in English.

Jim Cryer's translation of Han-shan Te-ch'ing's quatrain set reveals each poem to be a separate facet of the infinitely faceted jewel of Buddhist enlightenment. Not Wang Wei nor Han Shan wrote a better poem than this.

The Ch'ing was the second and the longer of China's two conquest dynasties. The Manchus, tough horse barbarians of the rich area northeast of China, regarded themselves as heirs to a kingdom in north China their ancestors had occupied in the closing years of the Sung, before they were unceremoniously tossed out by the Mongols. They admired the material luxury of Chinese civilization, and the capacity for the maintenance of it that was displayed by the Confucian bureaucracy, so after a historical accident and their own ferocity gave them dominion over China, they employed classically trained Chinese officials to perform all governing functions except the highest. Thus, for three centuries the Chinese official class were, however they rationalized it, collaborators, tools of an alien conqueror. It is no surprise that there is even less good poetry produced by this class than by its counterpart in Ming. I offer work by a Ming loyalist, Ku Yen-wu; by an "outsider" (maybe only after he bumped into the Manchu version of the glass ceiling), Yuan Mei; and by two Zen monks, one of whom was known for his anti-Manchu sentiments and the other of whom, like Yuan Mei, was also an outsider. Finally, I offer two poems by a fine poet, Fan Tseng-hsiang (1846–1931), an official who served the Manchus and the common people under his control honestly, living a lively life well into the republican period of the twentieth century.

Of these poets, it is seems surprising that the best two, Yuan Mei and the monk Ching An, are certainly among the best of all the classical Chinese poetic tradition. Both are outstanding for their mastery of classical forms and their willingness to use those forms to record the realities of their lives in a language that made classical poetry available to ordinary people. Both poets, a century apart, realized that the millions of readers of popular fiction were a potential audience for classical poetry; and so, unlike the majority of "classical" poets of the period, both refused merely to imitate the great poetry of the ancients, choosing rather to put classical techniques at the service of vernacular language, in order to reach the people, always the intended audience for *wen*. It's nice of them to have let me end this survey on other than a dying fall.

Mei Yao-ch'en (1002–1060)

A *Lone Falcon above the Buddha Hall of the Temple of Universal Purity*

From the house I just rented, you can see the temple,
gold and blue-green jade, before my broken down hut:
every day I watch the temple's flocks of pigeons,
perched or nesting, feasting even in this famine year.
Carved eaves and painted walls are covered with bird droppings,
and even the heads and shoulders of the Buddhas . . .
The monks wouldn't dare loose an arrow at them.
Then suddenly, the falcon, cruel claws spread,
and crows caw, magpies screech, and mynah birds cry out.
The raging falcon, coming on, catches the scent of flesh.
The falcon's heart is hot and hard: he fears no flock.
In an instant he's crushed a bird's head, and the rest flee
         in panic.
The dead bird's falling, but before it reaches earth,
flashing wings, a whirlwind dives to catch it,
and standing alone on the rooftop, tears it apart,
ripping the flesh, pecking out the liver, letting the guts
         drop away.
Scavengers, artless schemers, cowards all:
circle, aching to come close, their hungering eyes transfixed by
         the scene.
Soon enough the falcon's satisfied; he flies away.
In the struggle for the leavings you can't tell kites from crows.
A crowd of kids stood pointing. Folks on the street just laughed.
I chanted this poem as I stood by the autumn river.

Liu Yung (fl. 1034)

"Where I gaze"

Where I gaze, the rain is ending
and the clouds break up,
as I lean at the rail in anxious silence
seeing off the last of autumn's glow.

The evening scene is lovely enough
to chill an ancient poet into sadness,
and though the touch of wind and rain is light,
the duckweed gradually grows older.

In the moonlit frost the *wu-t'ung's*
leaves whirl yellow.
Giving love is taking pain:
Where are you now?
The misty waters: vast, and vague.

Writing or drinking, it's hard to forget . . .
How many nights alone beneath the clouded moon?
Again the *changes*, stars and frost, seas broad,
the heavens far, and no way home.

Swallows pair, as I depend on letters.
I point into the evening sky, but
there is no returning boat.

At dusk we gaze at one another,
in the sound of the swans' cry,
standing till the slanting sun is set.

"On the road to Ch'ang-an"

On the road to Ch'ang-an my horse goes slowly.
In the tall willows a confusion of cicada cries.
Slanting sun beyond the isles,
and winds of autumn on the plain. Only
where the heavens hang,
the view cut off.

The clouds go back, but
gone, they leave no track.
Where *is* the past?
Unused to indulgence, a little
wine's no consolation.
It's not
as it was
when I was young.

"A *leaf this boat*"

A leaf this boat, its light sail rolled
lies moored by the Ch'u's south bank.
As dusk descends on the lonely wall, the post horn
draws mournful notes like those of a Tartar whistle.
The waters vast,
wild geese on flat sand
settle, startled, scatter.
Mist gathers in the cold woods,
the painted screen is spread,
horizon's far, the mountains small
like faintly traced eyebrows.

Old joys cast off lightly,
I'm here to seek an official post
but weary of this journeying
and the waning year.
The manners and the sights of this strange place
are desolate and mournful,
the eyes despair,
the capital's far away,
the towers of Ch'in cut off,
the soul of a traveler dismayed.
The fragrant grass spreads in
empty vastness
and the evening glow spreads
no news of her,
a few broken clouds
far off.

Ou-yang Hsiu (1007–1072)

"By the lake the bright red bridge"

By the lake the bright red bridge
sounds with the wheels of painted carriages.
The surge of spring is in the stream
and spring's clouds, like desire, rise,
yet the water's green as glass and polished clean,
a mirror clear of anything of earth's.
Drunk, and on the road, I am
bound in floating threads of spring.

Blossom hidden, a bird calls the traveler back.
The sun slants away as I return.
What's to be done with spring?

"Snow clouds are suddenly the blooming cumulus of spring"

Snow clouds are suddenly the blooming cumulus of spring.
I come aware the year's a flower fit to lead the eye
to northern branches where the plum buds brave the chill
      to open,
or southern shore where ripples wrinkle green as wine.

The fragrant grasses wait in turn to bloom.
I can't endure these feelings; no place to find relief.
Before my cup, I'll scheme a hundred schemes to bring
spring on, and won't, though spring wounds deep, sing sadly.

"You cannot hold it . . ."

You cannot hold it . . .
Pretty girls grow old
and indolent; there is an end to spring.
When breeze is warm and moon so fine,
if you can manage yellow gold, buy smiles.
Nurture the tender blossoms there, don't wait.
No flowers to be plucked
from empty bough.

"A painted skiff with a load of wine, and West Lake's good"

A painted skiff with a load of wine, and West Lake's good.
Urgent pipes and quarrelsome strings,
a jade cup demands attendance.
Afloat on peaceful seas,
I'll accept the post
of drunken sleeper.

Clouds float beneath the moving boat.
Empty waters: pure and fresh.
Look up, look down; stay, or go on.
There's another heaven
in this lake.

"A whole life of saying, West Lake's good!"

A whole life of saying, West Lake's good!
Now the people press about the carriage.
Wealth and honor? Floating clouds.
Look up, look down; the rushing years:
two decades.

I come back, old white head, ancient crane.
The people of the city and the suburbs,
all strange; all new.
Who'd recognize the old coot, their master, on another day?

"At the lookout, plum blossoms scattered"

At the lookout, plum blossoms scattered,
slender willows by the bridge above the stream.
Warm winds from misty grasses stirred your reins,
parting's sorrow rode beside you,
and yet it is not gone,
runs like a spring freshet, always on.

A small, a gentle sorrow,
yet a rush of staining tears.
The tower's high, I won't go near the railing.
Spring Mount's as far as I could see from here:
you've gone beyond there now.

"Face turned to falling flowers; a breeze,
ripples on the water"

Face turned to falling flowers; a breeze, ripples on the water.
Willows deep in mist again, a snow of catkins flying.
Rain gone, a light chill lingers.
Spring's sorrows mix with wine, and I grow sick and weary . . .
Blue-green ruff of bedclothes, flower of the lamp,
night after night I stare unstirring:
silent, I rise and lift the screen.
Bright moon just at the pear branch tip:
a pair, apart.

Swallow Falls

Swallows return here
to cold heights to dart through flying waters.
My friends gone, my heart sees them:
a flash of pure brilliance, glistening, long.

Far-Off Mountains

Mountain colors, up close, far off,
all day going, as I gaze at the crags.
Different peaks in view from every different place:
I will not know their names.

Returning in the Moonlight to Huang-hua

Joy's in the sound of the spring up the cliff,
evening late, the mountains quiet.
Pines, in a wash of moonlight,
a thousand peaks, a single hue.

Lang-ye Creek

Mountain snows melt, swell the stream.
I cross on a tree felled long ago.
No way to know the distance to the source:
watch it rush, from among mountain flowers.

Su Shih (1037–1101)

The Old Fisherman

I
Where does the *fisherman* go for a drink
when his fish and his crabs are all sold?
He never sets himself a limit: just keeps on drinking till he's drunk,
and neither he nor the bartender totes up his tab.

II

When the fisherman's drunk, his straw cloak dances,
searching through drunkenness to find the way home.
Light skiff, the short oars akimbo:
and when he wakes up he never knows where.

III

The fisherman's awakening: spring river's noon.
A dream cut short by falling petals, floating silks.
Wine awakened, drunken still, and drunk, he's still awake.
He smiles upon this world of men, both now and gone.

IV

The fisherman's smile: a seagull floating,
lost in a river of mist and rain.

By the riverside, on horseback, an official's come,
to hire his skiff, to ferry him on toward the south.

Spring Day

Pigeons coo: swallows feed their young without a sound.
Sun's rays through the window westward make everything
      come clear.
Sobered up, at noon, and nothing to *do*,
except maybe take a nap in this spring sunshine.

Two Poems on Paintings by Mr. Yin

I
A Toad

Bulging eyes: who you glaring at?
Who you bluffing, puffing that white belly out.
You'd better not bother a centipede . . .
How much less a hungry snake? He'd never leave you be.

II
A Snail

Not enough spit to fill your own shell,
barely enough to keep yourself damp.
You climbed too high: you'll never get back down again.
You'll just end up shriveled there, stuck on the wall.

To the Abbot of the Tung-lin Monastery

Sound of the stream: his broad long tongue;
colors of the mountains, the Buddha's body, pure.
In a single night the stream will sing
eighty-four thousand hymns of praise.
Some other day, will you lecture on them?

A Monk at Chi-hsien Temple Asked Me to
Name a Hall There

Past the eye: flourishing, withering, lightning and wind,
for *longevity* what's a match for red blossoms?
Where the abbot sits in meditation, he sees the hall, empty,
seeing what is, seeing what is empty: *is* is what is, empty.

"Wine at East Bank"

Wine at East Bank tonight, I sobered up
then started over, getting drunk again.
Got home, a little fuzzy, maybe close to three,
and the houseboy was snoring like thunder.
I knocked at my own gate, and nobody answered,
leaned on my cane and listened to the River running.

I hate it! that even this body's not mine alone . . .
Someday I'll give it *all* up.
The night moves, the breeze writes
quiet in the ripples on the water.

A little boat, leaving here and now,
the rest of my life, on the river, on the sea.

Presented to Liu Ching-wen

Lotus withered, no more umbrellas to the rain.
A single branch, chrysanthemum stands against the frost.
The good sights of the year: remember those,
and now too: citrons yellow, tangerines still green.

A Harmony to Ching Hui-shu's Rhymes

Bells and drums from the south bank of the river.
Home? Startled, I wake from the dream.
Clouds drift: so also this world.
One moon: this is my mind's light.
Rain comes as if from an overturned tub.
Poems too, like water spilling.
The two rivers compete to see me off;
In the treetops the slanting line of a bridge.

T'ien-ho Temple

Green tiles, red railings
from a long way off this temple's a delight.
Take the time to take it in,
then you won't need to look back, turning
your head a hundred times.

River's low: rocks jut.
Towers hide in whirling mist.
Don't roar, don't rail
against it. The sound would just fade
in that distance.

"Rapt in wine"

Rapt in wine against the mountain rains,
dressed I dozed in evening brightness,
and woke to hear the watch drum striking dawn.
In dreams I was a butterfly,
my joyful body light.

I grow old, my talents are used up,
but still I plot toward the return . . .
to find a field and take a cottage
where I can laugh at heroes,
and pick my way among the muddy puddles
on a lakeside path.

Li Ch'ing-chao (1084–c. 1151)
(Translated by James Cryer)

"Tired of swinging"

Tired of swinging, indolent I rise,
with a slender hand, put right my hair.

The dew thick on frail blossoms,
sweat seeping through my thin robe,
and seeing my friend come,
stockings torn, gold hairpins askew,
I walk over, blushing,
lean against the door, turn my head,
grasp the dark green plums and smell them.

Thoughts from the Women's Quarters

On her face, hibiscus lovely, an incipient smile.
Poised in flight, the jeweled duck's beak. Incense wreathed
eyes alight, beneath the quilt she suspects
his frivolity hides a more expressive depth;
folds his elegant letter,
places it next her secret heart.
When the moon has gone,
the flowers in shadow,
I will come again.

"On the lake"

On the lake the wind brings waves
from some watery reach.
Autumn is old, red blossoms few, fragrances slight.
The water is bright with the mountain's image.
Our intimacies, ceaseless talk, endless love.
Lotus seeds are ripe, leaves withered.
Bright dew bathes the duckweed flowers, the beach grass;
and gulls and egrets asleep on the sand

won't watch, as if they mourn
your early leaving.

"Out the window of my little house spring colors darken"

Out the window of my little house spring colors darken.
Shadows weigh heavily on the curtains.
Keeping to my room, silent, I tune my jade lute
as distant peaks emerge against the mountains,
evening hastens, a fine wind blowing rain dallies
in the shadows as the pear blossoms are about to die,
and I can't stop them.

"Fallen faded petals"

Fallen faded petals the color of my rouge . . .
One year, another spring,
willow catkins lightly fly, bamboo shoots become bamboo
and alone and sad I face the garden's new-sent green.
But though he's not done roaming, that time must be near.
In a clear dream of last year come from a thousand miles
cloudy city, winding streams, ice on the ponds
for a while I gazed on my friend.

Thoughts from the Women's Quarters

Utter stillness in my room, the inch of my heart
yielding to a thousands threads of sorrow,
for the spring I loved, the spring now gone.

A few drops of rain worrying the blossoms
as I lean a while on the railing,
the knot of love, not unwound.
Oh, where is he?
Day after day, flowers fading, my gaze has slipped
from the road he'll come.

Separation

Red lotus fragrance gone to autumn's pale bamboo,
I lightly free these silken robes,
going in my orchid boat.
There in the clouds someone's sent a loving note,
in lines of returning geese,
and as the moon fills my western chamber,
as petals dance over the flowing stream
again I think of you,
the two of us living, a sadness apart
a hurt that can't be removed.
Yet when my gaze comes down,
my heart stays up.

Late Spring

Last night rain spattered, the wind was violent.
Even deep sleep has not dispersed the lingering wine
and when I ask, as he rolls the curtains up,
Still is my begonia as before, do you know, do you know?
he replies,
The green leaves flourish, the red blossom fades.

Anonymous (dates unknown)

Drunken Villagers

The guest is drunk
and the host, and the boy,
and they sing, and they dance, and they laugh.
Who cares if you're thirty or fifty or eighty,
you bow politely, and he bows, and I . . .
No boisterous strings or mad flutes here to rush us.
We drink with the red rolling sun
till *he* falls in the west,
and pound time on our plates and our saucers and bowls
till they break.

Ali Hsi-ying (fl. late Yuan)

Lazy Cloud's Nest II

If someone came what would I do,
dozing here with my clothes on?
Completely at ease, feeling frisky . . .
Human life? What can you say?
Rank is above me a bit.
Wealth, I don't need it . . .

Ha ha, you laugh . . .
I laugh, ha ha.

Kuan Yun-shih (1286–1324)

Knowing Enough III

Flourishing and withering are fated.
Stop coveting, stop plotting.
Simply approach the thing in the cup.
Don't tell me Li Po's a sage.
Don't speak of Liu Ling's tomb.
Wine won't seep down
through the earth of their graves.

Lu Chih (1236–1306)

Bottle Gourd

Wine new strained, a gourd of spring wine on the island
where the cherry apple blooms.
A gourd unopened, yet its fragrant meaning clear . . .
I honor mounds of malt,
and snub the aristocracy.
Merry again . . .
This dreamscape's empty, false.
Chuang Chou dreamed he was a butterfly,
dreaming he was Chuang.

Feng Tzu-chen (fl. late Yuan)

At Ease in the Mountains

Moved to the peak of Ts'o-ngo Mountain:
sharp-witted woodsman,
but here the trees are never in flower,
leaves and branches in the wind and rain.

My friends all sing of the *"Return"*;
why go in the first place, I ask.
Here, outside the door, ten thousand cloudy mountains.
This place you cannot buy with blood-smeared cash.

Kuan Han-ch'ing (c. 1220–c. 1300)

Not Bowing to Old Age

I tease the clustering blossoms from the wall,
snap off the greening willow:
red as yet unopened bud,
slimmest, and most supple wand . . .
I'm a dandy! It's a rake I am,
trusting this hand that takes
the flower and the bough,

that I may bear the willow's withering, the flower's fall.
Half a life I've picked as I pleased,
half a life lain flower-eyed
entwined in tender limbs.

Commander in the dandies' army,
headman of the rakish hordes,
when I'm red-faced old I'll be the same,
spending my time on the flowers,
losing my cares in wine:
drinking and eating, carousing.
Punning and joking and playing with words,
I'm so smooth, just ripe,
with the rhymes and their rules!
There's no place in my heart
for mourning.

My companion's a girl with a silver guitar . . .
she tunes before the silver stage
and leans with a smile toward the door.

My companion's a spirit of jade.
I grasp her jade hand and jade shoulder
as she mounts my tower of jade.

My companion's "the Gold Hairpin Maiden."
She sings "The Gold Lock of Hair,"
offering the golden goblet up,
filling the floating golden cup.

You say I'm old, that I grow cold . . .
Don't think it!

I'm center stage, the boss,
trimmer than ever,

still slim and bold:
Commander-in-chief of the brocade troops
that throng this flowery encampment,
and I travel the districts
and wander the land for my sport.

Now your modern-day wastrel is nothing but that . . .
a pile of straw, or a hole in the sand, newborn bunny set loose for
      the hunt.
I'm the hoary blue pheasant
always slipping the noose
artful, dodging the net.

I've known the tramp of cavalry horses
and survived cold arrows from ambush . . .
I'll never fall behind.
Don't be telling me, "Comes middle age,
the game is up": I won't go gentle to my dotage.

I'm a bronze bean with a pure bell tone.
Steam me: I won't get tender.

Boil me: I won't be cooked.
Pound me: You can't make me bean paste.
Roast me: I'll never pop!

Who told you infants you could come in here
where the harlot weaves her brocade net
a thousand stories high, which can be hacked,

but not hacked out, chopped, but never down,
which may be loosened, is never quite undone,
may be discarded, but not for long?

I play beneath some storied garden's moon.
My drink is fabled Kaifeng wine.
My *current* love is a Loyang flower,
and I only pick the willows from Chang Terrace!

I can play *go*, and I can play football.
I'm a hunter (and a wag), I can
dance, and I can sing, and I
can play the flute. I spread
a rare table, and chant a fine poem.

(And I'm great at chess.)

You can knock out my teeth and break my jaw.
You can cripple my legs and rip off my arms:
let heaven lay all these curses on me,
and I still won't stop.
Except old Yama, the king of Hell
comes to call on me himself (and brings his fiends to fetch me),
when my soul turns to dirt,
and my animal shell falls straight into Hell,
then, and only then, I'll quit this flowered path
I ramble on.

"Great Virtue" Song

Toot once, strum once . . .
give us a song
          to Great Virtue.

Enjoy yourself, relax,
stop setting snares.
Get delicate
        and follow
where that leads you.
Go find yourself a place to flop
and flop there.

Autumn

This autumn scene's worth words' paint:
red leaves fill up the mountain stream.
The path through the pines is set just so.
Chrysanthemums glow gold around the eastern hedge.
I raise this very proper goblet, drain the dregs.
The commoner who offers you the cup's
fit for high post, but what's the use . . .
Get back . . .
I'll study T'ao Ch'ien, learn to be drunk
as he was.

_____

Fan K'ang (fl. late Yuan)

When you're always drunk,
what's past is no problem.
You'll ponder when you're not,
but what sense is there?
"Accomplishment" and "fame"?
I'll pickle them, and

drown a thousand years of ups and downs
in unstrained wine.
The endless rainbow of ambition
should be doused in yeast.
Failed, I'll laugh at Ch'u Yuan
for trying . . .
if you know music
you listen to T'ao Ch'ien.

Liu Shih-chung (fl. late Yuan)

Today one state, tomorrow another,
struggle how many risings and declines?
Try to count from the beginning through . . .
Each and every reign,
loyal and filial ministers,
wise and enlightened kings,
lie in the earth.

Ma Chih-yuan (1266?–1334?)

Stand at the peak,
let my head go naked.
In dying light weird shadows:
pine shade all confused,
clear pool almost a void.
The image of the moon drawn large.
Sea breeze: sunsets' clouds break up.

If I fall down drunk,
don't raise me.

Eight Little Verses: Get Back

Capped in wild flowers,
fondling a bottle of raw wine,
how could I worry?
You can't always ride, you'll
fast on occasion . . .
A little field, an ox, I'll eat
till I'm full.

◆

A will to help . . .
hand that grasps cloud.
I'm out of step, why be unbending,
flow through this banishment, why suffer?
A couple of quilts, a soft sheet, I'll lie
till I'm warm.

◆

Moon capped, star cloaked, going . . .
A lonely inn at All Souls . . .
No home till autumn.
Wife and child at home, secure,
I waste away.
Sadness on the couch, grief on horseback,
till I die.

◆

Good sons, chaste wives . . .
Machines to crush the heart.
In the end you cannot flee
their dying or their change.
Wrangle for profit, or fame?
Struggle for wealth, or place?
All foolishness.

◆

Just got a jug
and bought a fish . . .
My eyes are full of cloudy mountains
unrolling like a scroll.
No way to make poems of this . . .
fresh breeze, bright moon.
I'm just a lazy rambler,
got nothing to sell.
Got to get back.

◆

By greening cane,
among blue pines,
bamboo's shade, pines' whisper . . .
there's my hut.
The empire's at peace
within my idle body.
I'll tend to the paths.
I'll plant five willows like T'ao Ch'ien.
Got to get back.

◆

Once-lustrous hair falls out.
Fair features change.
I'd be ashamed to show
this muddy face in public,
but the garden's scene endures
the same.
A field, a house,
get back.

◆

Dawn, the mountain bird outside the window
calls the old man up from sleep.
Now he says, get back!
and then he says, there's no way there from here.
Better find a shady spot
and sit down on the ground.

Po P'u (c. 1220–c. 1300)

I've known glory, I've known shame:
I keep my mouth shut tight.
Who's right? Who's wrong?
I nod my head in silence,
as I ponder poems and histories.
I fold my hands, keep them clean.
I'm poor as can be,
yet elegant, and free:
the wind freely flowing . . .

Wine this morning, drunk by noon . . .
this finite cup is empty.
Some shore is promised to the turning head:
I turn and find cold sea.
Dust flies.
Suns set, moons wane:
My friends, white-haired, and few.

If wine doesn't get me then poetry must . . .
spirit wars with spirits, poetry with wine.
All year long I idle with the breeze and moon,
a useless man.
But poems and wine, the music
of the truth within.

Ch'en Ts'ao-an (dates unknown)

Five Verses

If you have wealth,
if you own things,
and have not grief or pain,
rejoice, don't be ungrateful.
No one lives a hundred years.
Seventy is many.
A clement man is richer than Shih Ch'ung.
Just close your eyes one morning,
and your fated turns are done.
Gold can change its master;
silver, too.

The storms of life are fierce indeed.
There's no sense talking of them.
The crane has long legs,
the duck has short,
and they're born beneath one heaven.
You so-called fishermen and woodsmen,
stop all that talk of what is saintly,
what is crude.
To find the way's an aid,
to lose it's loss.
Each is a saint;
each, a fool too.

◆

Soft yin repays yin.
Hard yang repays yang.
Take this to your bosom or
you'll labor, toil, hold nothing.
The wealthy man is evil omened,
one stroke of luck, and fortunes melt.
Men decay and pass away;
wealth, too.

◆

Do you wrinkle up your brow with grief?
The saint's prescription can cure you!
Liu Ling taught his closest friends . . .
when your bosom's full with sadness,

when your time has come to grieve,
his message comes in self-disclosing fragrance:
to know things change is fine but
not as good as
morning, evening
drinking wine.

◆

A worldly man, I sit
with a big glass tumbler full.
Pluck the lotus, peruse the dance, break into song.
Sing while I drink, see demons when I'm done.
All of this
so many motes of dust and chaff.
Men's rights and wrongs? I make the best of them.
Loftiness is possible;
lowliness, that too.

Chou Wen-chih (c. 1275–c. 1350)

Two Verses

When peach blossoms open in the court . . .
oh happy, joyous, drunk.
When lotus blooms perfume the pool . . . .
oh morning, evenings, drunk.
When golden asters cluster by the hedgerow path . . .
oh falling, tumbling, drunk.

And when the wax plum on the mountainside
first blooms to herald the spring . . .
oh coming, going, drunk.
Getting drunker, getting drunker,
Drunk and sober; sober, drunk.

◆

In spring I search the scent of bamboo
flowers by a stream, and drink . . .
in summer sail through lotus blossoms
by a willow-shrouded shore, and drink . . .
in autumn climb the aster path
to sit within a maple grove, and drink . . .
in winter snuggle by a rosy stove
in cozy hall, and drink . . .

Oh happiness, oh happiness
all four seasons, lovely scenes
and suitable for drinking.

Chang Yang-hao (1269–1329)

Four Verses

Before forty I quit my job
and came to tread the way of saints and sages.
If I come out, it's just because
I love the hills and streams.

My ears are clean . . .
My vision's ample . . .
When you ponder it,
this is true happiness
The golden girdle girds calamity.
Purple robe robes pain.
Are they better than my briar cane and cap of straw?

◆

I was young
and now somehow I'm old.
All of my life seems
like yesterday morning.
The glare and the shade,
the water running,
      and neither is clement.
It's better to get drunk, to sleep.
Let the sun and the moon handle rising and falling.
I'll pretend I know nothing.

◆

Ch'u Yuan's "sorrow" none can explain,
yet its meaning is clear as the sun and the moon.
The sorrow remains. The man is gone . . .
to feed the shrimp and crabs of the River Hsiang.
That gentleman was simply silly.
I'll stay in this green mountain shade,
singing wildly, and drinking till it hurts,
here's *joy* that's boundless.

◆

I live here retired, apart
from the dust of the vulgar.
Clouds and mist, it's peaceful.
A thousand mountains' green surrounds the hut:
I'm the old man in the painting.
Look at this limitless beauty . . .
Could I put it down
and serve again?

Chung Ssu-ch'eng (1275–1350)

Four Verses

Plucking ferns to eat in exile at Shou-yang
in vain enduring hunger,
wasn't that just silly quibbling?
Was Ch'u Yuan's sobriety
so much more grand than
T'ao Ch'ien's getting drunk?
Go find yourself a shady spot,
sit idle on the ground.

◆

Po Ya searched out his Chung Tzu-ch'i
to share the meaning in his music:
lute spoke to him of flowing streams and lofty hills . . .

Who knows my music so?
Go find yourself a shady spot,
sit idle on the ground.

◆

For eagle and sparrow the same sky to fly in . . .
Jade and pebbles are both stone . . .
How to divide in highs and lows?
Who cares what's true, what's false?
Go find yourself a shady spot,
sit idle on the ground.

◆

In his heart the taste of ashes . . .
Even the flavor of wine gone.
He's broken with his love, the cup,
he's left her bed and gone
to find himself a shady place:
sit idle on the ground.

———————————————

Yun-k'an Tzu (dates unknown)

Seven Verses

Chaos —
  pearl of no price,
where water's red, the harvest.
Muddy roiled but blinding bright,

held in the hand like the hand of a lover,
divine, divines,
against what passes in this world
for clever.

◆

No tricks,
        nothing doing:
the sun and moon endure their rush
and don't grow old.
Sail backwards?
Row against the flow?
To hell with that.
You'd better be known
for being quiet.

◆

Who envies you
oh high and mighty,
all done up in purple
and dangling your badge of rank?
My heart's at peace.
I'm satisfied with me.
There aren't many in the world today
to match *this* crafty rascal.

◆

Done with the world
and pure as darkness,

nothing to hold me, nothing restrain.
The old guy here within the grove,
before blue cliffs the moon's companion,
mad and singing, drunk and dancing,
smashed, polluted, with the wine
of endless life . . .

♦

These peaks and cliffs
are strange and rare,
blue pine and cypress all around.
It's quiet, few men pass.
A light-hearted sadness,
to live here
distant, at leisure.

♦

The flour's gone sour.
The grain in the bin has gone stale.
My ladle's busted, and even
my old begging bowl's got a harelip
No salt, just a couple of onions . . .
Contented heart's my portion; it's sweeter
than the sweetmeats of the world.

♦

Laugh if you want,
I understand.

So I've used up a fortune . . .
I've thought it over carefully,
and it doesn't bother me.
I'll just straggle down this road
till I've danced to some paradise . . .

Kao Ch'i (1336–1374)

A Walk on the East Bank of the River

Setting sun shines on half the river . . .
This time of day I take walks alone.
Sunset can deepen sadness:
but autumn purifies the poet's heart.
Birds peck a rotting willow:
Insects cling to its dying leaves.
I still feel homesick. Why?
Now that I've finally come home.

The Well of the King of Wu

It is said it mirrored palace ladies
As their jade-white hands pulled the well rope . . .
          flowers in the dew.
Now: the mountain's deserted; lone monk draws water.
A jarful of cold water: for flowers made offering to the Buddha.

Hsu Wei (1521–1593)
(Translated by James Cryer)

Cloud Gate Temple/Painting Plum Trees

Floating bridge
water flowing
the snow
spits
as I wander
late in March
the buds
now green
in trees
awash
with coldness,
but the only plum blossoms
to be seen
are in my painting.

Peach Leaf Ferry

I

In a book
seeing peach leaves
I thought of you
sadly   as if
you hadn't died.
Crossing now
at Peach Leaf Ferry

I see only
the river.

II

Sad
at Peach Leaf Ferry
for the green willows
graceful, delicate.
Ten feet of water,
five gallons of mud,
and their lovely reflections
can't be seen.

III

Sad
at Peach Leaf Ferry
confused reflections
of her face.
Ten feet of water
five gallons of mud
and her hairpin's fallen
where?

Painting Bamboo

Cheap silk
from Eastern Wu
dull and damp,

and too the pot
is bare
of sizing,
but when my brush
sweeps through
the shadow
of a solitary phoenix
here's silken rain
on the Hsiang Chiang River
and pale mists.

Dark Stream/An Album Leaf

Gold splashed
on a little fan,
the half full
moon.
In light charcoal
a dark stream
sketched,
a stream rushing
without sound,
just like
a lute
with the strings
unbound.

Crabs

Night
at the window

talking.
Fall River crabs
so plump
they deserve
a little drink.
Think I'll go
swap
a painting.

Chou Wen (dates unknown)

These few drops, these
tears of autumn on my heart.
I dare not let the first one fall
lest autumn's river well
on endlessly.

Chao Li-hua (dates unknown)

Farewell

My boat goes west, yours east.
Heaven's a wind for both journeys.
From here, the clouds and the mountains,
the horizon's vague.
A thousand miles . . .
My heart, a dark swan,
confused in that vastness.

Ma Shou-chen (dates unknown)

Since he's gone, he's gone.
There's no one else for this vessel of mine.
Wine, they say, melts sorrow.
How many times?

Hsu P'ien-p'ien (dates unknown)

Today you leave for Chiang-k'ou,
five days on Ch'ang-chou.
Alas, that these tears I shed for you
can't flow with the river beyond there.

Han-shan Te-ch'ing (1546–1623)
(Translated by James Cryer)

Mountain Living: Twenty Poems

I

Down beneath the pines,
a few thatched huts.
Before my eyes,
everywhere blue mountains,
and where the sun and moon
restless rise and fall,

this old white cloud
idly comes and goes.

II

When plum petals among the snows
first spring free
from the ends of night,
a dark fragrance flies
to the cold lantern
where I sit alone
and suddenly storms
my nostrils wide.

III

Through a few splinters of
white cloud, motionless,
the Buddha wheel bright moon
comes flying
to accompany me
in my mountain stillness . . .
and I smile up at it
above the dirty suffering world.

IV

It only took a single flake
to freeze my mind in the snowy night,

a few clangs to smash my dreams
among the frosted bells,
and the stove's night fire fragrance
too is melted away,
yet at my window the moon
climbs a solitary peak.

V

Through a face full of clear frostiness
raw cold bites.
Through a head overstuffed with white hair
a gale whistles.
And over the world from flowers of emptiness
shadows fall . . .
but from my eyes the spells of darkness
have completely melted.

VI

In the *sh sh* murmur of the spring
I hear
moon clear, the primal Buddha pulse
come from the West
with motionless tongue
eternally speak.
How can I be sad again?
How strange.

VII

In the dark valley
the orchid scent is overwhelming
and at midnight the moon's form
so gracefully sways by,
like a sudden flick of the
stag tail whisk . . .
reasonless it
smashes my meditation.

VIII

In its Buddha flash I forgot all,
reason quieted in contemplation
when an orphan brilliance glared on
my meditation, startling me
and I saw, off through the void,
lightning strike.
But it wasn't the same
as that firefly beneath my eyes.

IX

Clouds scatter the length of the sky,
rain passes over.
The snow melts in the chill valley
as Spring is born

and though I feel my body's like
the rushing water,
I know my mind's not
as clear as the ice.

X

I'm so rotted out
I should pity these weak bones.
But look! My consciousness is reborn,
my mind strengthens,
day and night my back
is like an iron rod.
Constant and pervasive is my meditation,
like an evening's frost

XI

In the empty valley
all filth is wiped away,
but this bit of lazy cloud
stays on.
For company I have the pine branches'
twitching stag tail whisks,
which is almost enough deer
to make a herd.

XII

Words,
an enchanted film across the eyes.

Ch'an,
floating dust on the mind.
Yet all ins and outs become one
with one twirl of the lotus
and the chilocosm
whole in my body.

XIII

A quiet night
but the bell toll will not stop
and on my stone bed dreams and thoughts
alike seem unreal.
Opening my eyes
I don't know where I am,
until the pine wind sounds
fill my ears.

XIV

Like some pure clarity
distilled out of a jeweled mirror,
the Spring waters
fill the many lakes,
reflect up into my eyes
here on Mt. Lu,
and the moon above my forehead
becomes a bright pearl.

XV

Six on the lotus clock?
The stick's too short
and on the incense piece . . .
where's the century mark?
Day and night are truly constant
and stop nowhere.
To know immortality in the morning
hold in your hand the womb of the flower to be.

XVI

Though a slice of cloud
seals the valley mouth
a thousand peaks
scratch open its emptiness
and in the middle
are a few thatched huts
where hidden deep is
this white-haired mountain man.

XVII

What a pity the blue mountains
go on forever.
This old white hair is petrified
of the time to come,
and plans to burn himself out
amongst the inns down in the dust.

Anyway, who ever heard
of a lazy transcendental?

XVIII

On the mountainside,
mournfully sipping the night rain
to the pine sounds,
throat choking on clear frost,
gone to beg food,
this Buddha's priest is a tired bird
and the moth brow crescent
moon arises new made up.

XIX

The world shines
like a watery moon.
My body and mind
glisten like porcelain
though I see the ice melt,
the torrents descend,
I will not know
the flowers of spring.

XX

Outside my door
blue mountains' bouquet.

Before my window
yellow leaves rustle.
I sit in meditation
without the least word,
and look back to see
my illusions completely gone.

Ku Yen-wu (1613–1682)

Ching-wei

The world is full of iniquities,
why do you struggle so in vain,
always urging on that tiny body,
forever carrying sticks and stones?
"I will fill up the Eastern Sea.
My body may fail; my aim won't change.
Until the great sea's filled
my heart can't know surcease."
Alas, don't you see
the many birds with sticks and stones among the Western Hills?
Magpies come, swallows go, all building their own nests.

Eight Feet

Eight feet tall, the lonely mast on this leaflet of a skiff.
With the wind, upon the water, it's carried me to this autumn.
We've been to White Emperor Town to search for our late ruler,
then east of the river to ask about one Chung-mou.

Even in the sea, the fish and dragons know our anguish;
in the hills, the trees wail forth their grief.
I trust you'll speak no more of "rise and fall";
the boatman of another year is white-haired now.

Yuan Mei (1716–1798)

Talking Art

In painting it's catching the "spirit" and "essence."
In poems that's "nature" and "feelings."

An elegant dragon, with its life's breath gone?
Better a rat, with some scurry left in him.

Climbing the Mountain

I burned incense, swept the earth, and waited
    for a poem to come . . .

Then I laughed, and climbed the mountain,
    leaning on my staff.

How I'd love to be a master
    of the blue sky's art:

see how many sprigs of snow-white cloud
    he's brushed in so far today.

Spring Day III

A hermit's gate is made of the stuff of brooms,
but sweep as it may, the clouds won't stay away.
So up through the clouds, for sun I came,
with wine, to this high tower.

At evening, the sun declined
to come on down the mountain with me.
"Tomorrow," I asked,
"you coming, or not?"

So Be It

Blossoms of apricot will perish,
sound of the rain grow quiet.

Moss in the footprints on the path,
its green reflected on my gown.

Wind's fierce,
can't keep the little window shut. . . .

Fallen flowers, pages of poems
together fly away.

Ginseng

I love a good logical chat about ethics,
but I won't sit still for a sermon.

Purple Mountain Ginseng's best:
it works, and it doesn't taste so bad.

Speaking My Mind

I

When the clouds come the mountain
        "ontologically dismanifests."
When they go (I guess) it exhibits its
        phenomenological "mountainness."
Do you suppose
        the mountain knows?

II

Oh, perhaps the fabled P'an Ku made the world,
but before the Farmer Spirit had tilled one field,
bored to death with the time on his hands,
the Great Fu Hsi brushed the single stroke
of the first written word. He's the one
who really got things going.

III

To learn to be without desire
        you must desire that.
Better to do as you please:
        sing idleness.

Floating clouds, and water running . . .
>   where's their source?
In all the vastness of the sea and sky,
>   you'll never find it.

Laughing at People Who Complain about the Heat

Don't complain of the hot summer winds,
they'll blow themselves away, at last.
And don't just sit there waiting for the autumn's cool.
That's a fine sure way to shorten your life.

Late Gazing, Looking for an Omen as the Sun Goes

I

The window's dark. Roll back the curtain's waves.
What's to be done about sunsets?
Climb up and stand in some high place,
lusting for a little more twilight.

II

From a thousand houses' cooking fumes,
the Changes weave a single roll of silk.
Whose house, fire still unlit, so late?
Old crow knows whose, and why.

III

Golden tiles crowd, row on row:
men call this place the Filial Tombs.
Across that vastness, eyes wander:
grand pagoda: one wind-flickering flame.

The Bell

Ancient temple, monks all gone,
the Buddha's image fallen.

The single bell
hangs high in evening's glow.

Sad, so
full of music . . .
Ah, just one little tap!
But no one dares.

Near Hao-pa
(I saw in the mist a little village of a few tiled roofs, and
joyfully admired it)

There's a stream, and there's bamboo,
there's mulberry, and hemp.
Mist-hid, clouded hamlet,
a mild, a tranquil place.

Just a few tilled acres.
Just a few tiled roofs.

How many lives would I
have to live, to get
that simple?

Gone Again to Gaze on the Cascade

A whole life without speaking,
    "a thunderous silence"
that was Wei-ma's way.

And here is a place where no monk can preach.

I understand now what T'ao Ch'ien, enlightened,
said he couldn't say.

It's so clear, *here, this water,*
    my teacher.

Chang-chou

I'm not such a goose that I live on the water . . .
but day after day my light sail slides by the shallows.
Even the reeds know the Great Official's here,
following the winds of custom,
they see me off
                 with a *boatful* of blossoms.

Willow Flowers

Willow flowers, snowflakes, the same . . .
they're feckless.

No matter whose garden they fall in,
they'll always follow the wind away.

*Finished with a Long Parting Poem to Mr. Li,
I Went On to Write This Shorter One*

Life is harder than our dreams,
but both, at last, come down to chance.
Poems repay no debts . . .
They may but show a little of the heart.
When I turned to look back at the river and the hills,
words of a poem from *The Poetry Classic* came to me
"Lo, he is right in the middle of the waters" . . .
and thinking of you, I chanted them once,
and then once again.

In Idleness

Rain gone, and one cicada sings.
On the empty veranda I sit, full of feeling.
"Men waste away," the wild geese cry.
"Blossoms age," the bees hum.
The winding waters song's the joy of solitude:
lofty is for mountains, not for men.

At last *to lead:*
my wife, my children, by the hand
into some wilderness
to till my own small kingdom.

Ah Chen

Ah Chen is ten, her hair still in pigtails . . .
She's read both Odes and the History,
(and her needlework's just fine).
Her mother scolds her, while her father smiles:
for the scion of whose House, I wonder,
did we take this burden on?

Cold Night

Cold night, reading,
forgetting sleep,
The embroidered coverlet has lost its fragrance,
and the brazier's cold.

My lady swallows her anger, but
snatches the lamp away
and asks me,
      "Do you know what time it is?"

Reading

When I shut a book,
I can be at ease.

If I open one, I agonize.
Books are long, and days are short,
feeling like an ant
who wants to move a mountain,
or a man who waits for dawn light
with a candle in his hand.

Of ten I read, I might remember one.
The more's the pain,
that in a thousand years
there'll be more books, no end.

So if I wish I were a spirit-being,
or pray Heaven for a few more years . . .
it's not that I want to dine on dew,
or wander fairylands . . .
every word that's written,
to read each one, that's all.

On a Painting of a White-Haired Old Man

Who'd paint a white-haired ancient?
I smile. I'd rather be a *duck*.
If you're born with your head snow-white already,
no one can laugh and shout, "You're getting old!"

Sixty

Each year as the year day's passed
I've cocked my ear to hear

the fireworks pop, so sharp, so clear,
all through the night till dawn.

This year I didn't listen,
fearing the cock crow's news:
my sixtieth year.

The noise has died now,
to the sound of a page of the calendar turning.
A little time's left. Maybe, just a scrap?

The cock, at least, shows sympathy,
so slow to crow for me.
That's fine. I'll just go on
being fifty-nine.

Remembering

The years, their months
turn, grave and slow, their
fall and spring, again.

Mountain flowers, mountain leaves and
each time's new.

Sometimes I sit alone
and smile upon the child I was,

in memory now distant
and a friend.

Conscious of Withering

"Oh, verily, I wither," said Confucius of himself,
and even a thousand of his words
aren't worth one picture of me.
Teeth falling out, the hair at my temples
like feathers molting.
I drag my staff among the flowers,
squint right beneath the lamp at normal print,
inclined to forget what I know I ought to note,
grown accustomed to blithering on, and on, and on.
"Ah, how it passes, it passes away," the stream
of life, I heard the Master say.
        And of the saying, "the older the better,"
        now that's a stupid one.

Memories

Young, I loved to read good books:
word for word I memorized whole chapters.

Old, I love to read good books:
to pass the time, to follow where my interest leads me.

Although it's true I forget half I read,
what passes my eyes is all mine.

The flavors in a book I savor,
better by far than any vintage wine.

Unable to Sleep, I Was Inspired to Write This

Old, spirit shriveled, sleepless nights,
no way of knowing how many dawns I've seen.
If there was anyone to beg,
I'd beg a trip to Dreamland.
I'd rather dream one single dream
than live another year.

Answer to a Letter Inquiring about My Health

When a man's about to quit this world
the changes in his habits often show it.
The drinker may perhaps set down the cup,
the wanderer's step grow slow.
It's been *my* nature to love company:
let anyone show up, we're off and gabbing.
But since this last illness began,
a single peep and I cover my ears . . .
to the point that when the wife and children
come to pay respects, I wave them off, and nothing more.
I know that's ominous: this old body's clearly nearly done for.
So who would guess how I dote on my old writings;
happily, delightedly, there's one vice I still enjoy.
I made a poem in the middle of my illness,
a loud chanting that the night couldn't stop.
Does this line here take a "push" or a "knock"?
I'm Chia Tao once again, revising every line
from head to tail. All I really want

is to make every phrase come alive, I
won't countenance one dead word.
Well . . . maybe the fact that this habit remains
with this vestige of a body
means there's some time left to it too.

Last Poem: Goodbye to My Garden

Was I no more than some fairy-being,
strange beast from the Sutra of Ceylon,
arisen and set free to play
in Hsiao-ts'ang's summit garden?

Did I not know that garden's guests
of poems and lutes, wine and songs
would also hear the gong of time,
the last dripped drop of the water clock?

My eye roams the towers and pavilions,
and I know these lines are my farewell.
This mountain full of birds will stay,
forever wound and bound in its flowers.

Long ago an Immortal chose to return
to his home in the form of a crane,
and was almost shot down by a lad with a sling.
If I ever come back to this Paradise,
I'll remember to be careful.

Ching An (1851–1912)

Dusk of Autumn: Writing What My Heart Embraces

I am the orphan cloud: no trace left behind.
Come south three times now to listen to the frosty bell.
When men see geese flying, they think of letters home.
Even the mountains grieve at the fall: they're wearing a sickly face.
But fine phrases are there too, to be plucked from the sad heart
       of autumn,
and many an ancient poet ran into one on the road.
I'm ashamed I've yet to realize my monk's oath:
the fault's in this load of blue green hills I carry,
many tens of thousands strong.

Facing Snow and Writing What My Heart Embraces

At Mount Ssu-ming in the cold in the snow,
half a lifetime's bitter chanting.
Beard hairs are easy to pluck out one by one:
a poem's words are hard to put together.
It's *pure vanity*, to vent the heart and spleen;
words and theories, sometimes, aren't enough.
Loneliness, loneliness; that's my everyday affair.
The soughing winds pass on the night bell sound.

To Show You All, on the First Morning of the Year

A thousand thousand worlds, a single breath,
one turn of the Great Potter's Wheel.

The withered tree blossoms in a spring beyond illusion.
Pop!
The firecrackers bring me back: the laugh's on me.
This year's man
                    is last year's man.

Beating the Heat at Jade Lake

West of the painted bridge east of the willow's shade:
ten *li* of flat lake: water touching, holding, sky.
Not like it is among men, bitter at the burning heat.
Monk's robe sits idle: lotus blossoms: breeze.

Night Sitting

The hermit doesn't sleep at night:
in love with the blue of the vacant moon.
The cool of the breeze
that rustles the trees
rustles him too.

Over King Yu Mountain with a Friend

Sun sets, bell sounds, the mist.
Headwind on the road, the going hard.
Evening sun at Cold Mountain.
Horses tread men's shadows.

On a Painting

A pine or two,
three or four bamboo,
cliffside cottage, long, solitary, silence.
Only floating clouds come to visit.

Moored at Maple Bridge

Frost white across the river, waters reaching toward the sky.
All I'd hoped for's lost in autumn's darkening.
I cannot sleep, a man adrift, a thousand miles
alone, among the reed flowers: but the moonlight fills the boat.

At Hu-k'ou, Mourning for Kao Po-tzu

Though he was young, Kao
was the crown of Su-chou and Hu-k'ou.
It was only to see if he was still here
that I came today to this place . . .
found a chaos of mountains.
No word. This evening sun. This loneliness.

Laughing at Myself I

Cold cliff, dead tree, this knobby-pated me . . .
still thinks there's nothing better than a poem.

I mock myself, writing in the dust, and
damn the man who penned the first word
and steered so *many* astray.

Laughing at Myself II

Slices of flesh made burnt offering
to the Buddha . . .
Just so, I came to know myself
a ball of mud, dissolving in the water.
I had ten fingers. Now, eight remain.
Did I really think I could become a Buddha
one slice at a time?

Su Man-shu (1884–1918)

Written at White Cloud Ch'an Hall
Beside West Lake

Where white clouds are deep, Thunder Peak lies hidden.
A few chill plums, a sprinkle of red rain.
After a fast, oh so slowly . . .
the mud in my mind settles out.
The image in the pool before the hut:
fallen from that far-off bell.

Passing Rushfields

Where the willow shade is deep . . .
the water chestnut flourishes.
Endless, silver sands . . .
where the tide's retreated.
Thatched booths with wine flags flapping
tell me there's a market town nearby.
A whole mountain of red leaves:
a girl child carries kindling.

Passing the Birthplace of Cheng Ch'eng-kung's Last Loyal Defender of the Ming

A passerby points far off and says,
"That's Lord Cheng's Rock."
White sand, green pines, beside the setting sun
as far as you can see,
how many loyal sons of China left?
Monk's robe, and tears, bow down
before the memorial stone.

Headed East, Good-bye to an Elder Brother

Rivertown's a picture
run from our overturned cups.
Together just a moment, this time:
how many times harder to part?
From here the lone boat, the night,
bright moon.

Parting the clouds, who'll gaze out
from high upon the tower?

Fan Tseng-hsiang (1846–1931)

Random Verses from a Boat I

Three days, and we've changed boats twice.
Now, they say, it's Hsi-ch'uan County.
Smoke from kitchen fires is thick.
The city walls in good repair again.
We hear the county's government is all set right,
and the common folk applaud the magistrate's decisions.
On the eastern shore the grain grows glossy green.
A hundred pennies buys a peck of flour . . .
In Chengchou, this same river burst its dikes.
Both groves and marshes are full of homeless folk:
there, they're geese, grounded, or looking more like stranded fish,
while here the people are safe as swallows nesting in the eaves.
These are both the people of Yu-chou;
but thirty miles divides calamity from joy.
Like fruits of the same grove,
sweet and sour growing side by side.
Here many are at peace, at leisure;
there, the toilers, that eternal moan.

Random Verses from a Boat II

Before dawn, we passed Chiang-k'ou town,
waters swift as arrows flying.

With the River of Stars astern on the right,
my boat passed the most marvelous sight on the left:
Standing alone in the flow of the river,
a peak like a lotus, elegant, the single flower.
And then these little islets:
green conch shells in a silver bowl . . .
Long ago I fell in love with Little Orphan,
I've sailed past it at least ten times.
a flowered islet hung amid the flow,
wreathed all about in misty waves.
This little peak so much like that:
call it Taoist magic, Soul Travel, brought it here for us!
It's five years since I left Chiu-kiang,
and now Heaven sends its best sight here!
Too bad there's no way to anchor;
swift shallows rush the light barge down.
I turn, gaze back upon the coiffure of the mist,
at Heaven's edge, its vast and supple grace!

Notes

PART ONE: *From Before: The Beginning*

"The Peasant's Song," p. 11: Both the Confucian Mencius (372–288 B.C.E.) and his contemporary the Taoist Chuang Tzu (c. 360 B.C.E.) attest that this is "the first Chinese poem." From this evidence we can only know that the work preceded at least one of the two who cite it, the other of whom might or might not even have been its author. It is very unlikely that it is actually older than all of the poems in the *Shih Ching*, but its theme of independence and individuality is as old as the hills (and valleys, and swamps) in which the peasants lived.

"My Lord Is Full of Yang," p. 18: The pun on organ (a reed pipe, a mouth organ) is there in the original. The *Yang* of the *Tai-chi*, the well recognized picture of *Yin* and *Yang* in their eternal embrace, does refer in traditional Chinese culture to the male member, as well as to the principle of maleness, and to the sun, among other related ideas.

"Before the East Was Bright," p. 19: This poem is alluded to in T'ao Ch'ien's "Drinking Wine" set, p. 58–62, and it is clear there as here that both the court officer's anxious desire to please and the duke's disorderly demands are being satirized. T'ao Ch'ien's poem is stronger because he uses the time-honored poem from the sacred classic to satirize himself.

"No Clothes," p. 19: A recruiter seeks to shame shirkers and welcome brothers-in-arms. Less subtle techniques of recruitment are seen in Tu Fu's "The Press-Gang at Shih-hao Village," p. 110.

"Li Sao," p. 27: "at dusk I sup the fallen petals of chrysanthemum . . ." The autumn chrysanthemum will serve as an allusion to this passage wherever it reappears in later Chinese literature. See, for instance, T'ao Ch'ien's "Drinking Wine," number 5, p. 58. The verb translated as "sip" in the line above the chrysanthemum is the same verb translated as "drinking" in the T'ao Ch'ien set.

"Li Sao," p. 27: Ch'u Yuan rephrases the statement, "I depend upon, and may well end upon, P'eng Hsien's model," as an oath in the final line of the poem.

"Li Sao," p. 28: In the original the poet puns on the name of the Chou dynasty several times. I have raised the second level of meaning into the foreground, in the belief that for Ch'u Yuan's readers it was abundantly clear that he intended to mock the northern culture, as well as the tendency of the court faction of the state of Ch'u to mimic Chou manners and mores. It's not surprising, I think, that since the appropriation of this text to the Confucian tradition, the mockery of Chou has been left uncommented upon in China.

"Li Sao," p. 28: Note the constant wordplay surrounding the word *way*. Beginning here and continuing into the twentieth century in classical poetry, at least, the term almost always has multiple significances in poetry, meaning the Confucian Way, the Taoist and the Buddhist Way, and simply a route, road, or way of getting on. Echoing a popular misreading of the first line of the *Tao Te Ching* of Lao Tzu, the character is sometimes also used to mean "to speak."

"Li Sao," p. 29: "Let my hat be a tower . . ." Pride in purity of purpose combines with the ideal of loyal service to the people, through the legitimate Lord, to make the *Li Sao* an obvious object of appropriation by the Confucians of the dynasties post Chou.

"Li Sao," p. 29: The Yuan dynasty poet and popular dramatist Kuan Han-ch'ing alludes to the line beginning "Let me be carved . . ." in his own egotistical, romantic, and hyperbolic fashion in his "Not Bowing to Old Age," p. 175.

"The Fisherman's Song," p. 38: The "hat strings" have traditionally been taken to refer to the strings that hold the hat of office on the head. Thus the meaning is something like, "When the times are right, I can serve the state as all good men should. When the times would require I be morally compromised by service, I may retire into hermitage." Ch'u Yuan is a hero for the Confucian and a fool for the Taoist. Most traditional Chinese literati were both Confucian and Taoist. The difficulty posed by this paradoxical advice is apparent in the allusion made to this poem in major works by such poets as T'ao Ch'ien, Wang Wei, and Li Po.

"Song at Kai-hsia," p. 39: Hsiang Yu, at least pretender to the position of prince of Ch'u, was most likely literate and may indeed have written this poem. It seems more likely that it was written anonymously and posthumously by a Ch'u loyalist to create a romantic aura around the figure of the vanquished contender for the throne of a new dynasty.

"Song of the Great Wind," p. 40: This poem was performed to celebrate the destruction of the Ch'in Dynasty and the proclaiming of the first truly successfully unified Chinese dynasty, the Han. Liu Pang was a peasant and no doubt at best barely literate. Nonetheless, he chose brilliant associates and was a better military leader than all his rivals at least partly because he understood that success depended on the people's understanding that his victory would make their lives better. The concerns of a ruler, not just a war chief, are apparent in this poem. Its attribution to his name by traditional historians shows their desire to capture this vigorous and virile character (he once pissed in the hat of a prissy Confucian scholar who volunteered to design the proper ceremonial rites) within the confines of the concept of *wen*, making him properly suited to rule according to the dominant Confucian ideology of the period.

"Nineteen Old Poems of the Han," poem 2, p. 41: All previous translations have ignored the word *lattice*. I believe it is an allusion to a famous passage in the *Analects* of Confucius in which Confucius, barred from entering the sickroom, reaches through a window lattice to take the hand of an honored friend who is suffering from a terrible disease (commentators have assumed leprosy). Confucius says, "That such a man should suffer such an illness . . . " The wonderfully sophisticated presentation of the plight of a woman (who in conventional terms might be seen as "merely" a prostitute, perhaps frustrated in her schemes to raise herself out of "such an illness") is signaled by the allusion. The first six lines of the poem include doubled adjectives that engage the reader's imagination in a way that expands and diffuses the meaning of the doubled word. When the phrases appear in later poetry, they are most often allusions to this poem. Dictionaries often define the terms by reference to their context in this poem. The last line of the poem is worldly, knowing, and, I believe, sympathetic.

"Nineteen Old Poems of the Han," poem 10, p. 43: The poem presents the myth of the Herd Boy and the Weaving Girl, celestial lovers separated by the Emperor of Heaven and allowed only a single night a year, the seventh of the seventh (lunar) month.

What separates them is the Milky Way, which in Chinese has several names; here simply the Han River (an actual river on earth, too), elsewhere the river of stars or the river of the sky. Many if not most English translators fudge this one, some giving up all the river imagery for the sake of the idiomatic English of the Milky Way.

"Nineteen Old Poems of the Han," poem 13, p. 44: The Yellow Springs: from the earliest to the latest classical literature a rather nonspecific abode of the dead.

"Nineteen Old Poems of the Han," poem 13, p. 44: The great Li Po alludes to the image of life as wandering in one of his most famous lines, in "To the Tune of *P'u-sa-man*" [p. 96–97].

"Nineteen Old Poems of the Han," poem 13, p. 44: Taoist alchemists attempted to discover the "elixir of life." Many of their early inventions contained toxic chemicals, particularly mercury.

"Nineteen Old Poems of the Han," poem 17, p. 45: The position of the constellations in the sky at a certain time on any given night tells the sky watcher the time of year, just as their movement over the course of a minute or an hour tells a more ephemeral time. Living a more outdoor and less well-lighted life than we do, the traditional poets knew and used the skies to allude to many aspects of the passage of time.

PART TWO: *A Time of Trials*

"Fought South of the City Wall," p. 53: China's philosophies do, indeed, honor a pacifistic stance. However, neither Confucius nor Taoists advise accepting defeat. China is not, moreover, without her martial heroes and heroines.

Poems of Juan Chi, p. 54–57: These poems are drawn from Juan's eighty-two poems in pentameter, called the *Yung Huai Shih*

(Songs of My Heart's Ideals). The poet and his work are idols for T'ao Ch'ien, considered one of China's greatest poets, who also lived under a decadent government. Many phrases from Juan Chi's poems appear in T'ao's work.

"Poem 73," p. 56: This poem is loaded with references to the Taoist classic *Chuang Tzu*. For Tung-ye Chi and his horses, see *The Essential Chuang Tzu*, p. 109 (translated by J.P. Seaton and Sam Hamill, Shambhala Publications, 1998).

Poetry of Hsieh Ling-yun, pp. 65–67: I find that in spite of my personal prejudice against aristocracy (any "aristocracy": didn't our revolution send those *twits* who think they were *born* better than us plain folks back where they came from), something that I'm proud of and used to think of as the heritage of every American, *in spite*, I say, *of that prejudice*, when I came to translating a short selection from Hsieh Ling-yun I discovered a grudging admiration for the poet. My first introduction to Hsieh Ling-yun, as my heart and mind recall it, was in a lecture by a well-known native Chinese professor from a well-known Chinese literary family, which included several stories apparently from the scholarly "oral tradition" since I've never seen anything quite like them in print in Chinese or English since. These stories characterized Hsieh as an abusive "Lord" and a self-abusive drug user who, according to the storyteller, was often portrayed as looking something like the cartoon caveman Allie Oop, with lower legs that got broader and broader from the knee down, the result of edema caused by the recreational use or abuse of psychotropic mushrooms and ergot (grain rust fungus) derivatives. With this picture in mind, you may find the arrogant aristocrat of my prejudice in both the poems here selected.

PART THREE: *The Golden Age*

Buddhism in the golden age, p. 73: Contrary to popular misconception, Buddhism was never monolithic in China (or elsewhere, except perhaps at the very beginning). Three major Buddhist "churches," T'ien T'ai, Hua Yen, and Ch'ing T'u, along with several strong tantric sects, existed in T'ang China. Ch'an, or Zen, was actually born and nurtured toward maturity by T'ien T'ai in the eighth century.

"Palace Lament," p. 85: The willow is doubly powerful in reminding her of her mistake: breaking a twig is a ritual of parting, since the name of the tree is in Chinese a pun on a word that means "to stay" (to remain) and (in her afterthought) "to be detained." She should have had him stay. Now he "stays" somewhere else.

"Bamboo Pavilion," p. 85: The character for "again" in line 2 is the same character as that used in Wang Wei's next poem, "Deer Park." In both cases it alludes to the *I Ching*, one of the more subtle of the Confucian classics, where it means not just "again" but rather "to begin again at the beginning." Also note the similarity of the last line of this poem to the last line of Li Po's "Sitting at Reverence Mountain." A golden age may be necessarily full of poetic inspirations and friendly competition.

"Deer Park," p. 85: Both Chinese and English language poems are in fact multimedia artifacts, but the Chinese poet sometimes makes use of extra visual layers not directly available to his English language counterpart. For a rather wild ride through the poetic possibilities embodied in the original, see my essay "Once More, on the Empty Mountain," in *The Poem Behind the Poem: Translating Asian Poetry*, edited by Frank Stewart, Copper Canyon Press, 2004.

"To Magistrate Chang," p. 89: In English, this is probably Wang Wei's second most famous poem. What has often been read as a sort of Zen koan offered as advice from the wise old gentleman to the aspiring young official is by its reference to "The Fisherman's Song" transformed into a clear statement of Wang Wei's actual position. The poem then may appear somewhat sarcastic, since young Mr. Chang, a military official, was probably not sufficiently well educated to be able to appreciate the advice. Like some Taoists and many Zen teachers, Wang Wei does not seem to favor *gentle* guidance.

"Drinking with a Hermit Friend," p. 90: When you first read this poem in the Chinese, the thing that jumps out at you is the second line. In the characters, it's one cup, one cup, again, one cup. What dullness, or what daring? "A horse, a horse, my kingdom for a horse." Only a Li Po, or a Shakespeare, could get away with that kind of repetition. In Li Po's line we also find the playful use of the hyperclassical word for "beginning again," from the *I Ching*, that Wang Wei used in his "Deer Park." Li Po raises the stakes with the next line, however. It's a direct quote, with only one of the seven characters slightly changed, from the official biography of T'ao Ch'ien, in the *Sung Shu* (the history of Liu Sung dynasty, 420–477). This supposedly drunken song contains not only drunken babbling—"a cup a cup anutha cup"—but a wonderfully playful "scholarly" allusion as well.

"Sitting at Reverence Mountain," p. 90: Reverence Mountain is a "literal" translation of the name of the mountain, sometimes left untranslated as Ching-t'ing Shan. It is clear that Li Po is playing with the name.

"Thoughts of a Quiet Night," p. 90: The twenty characters of the original quatrain include two that are stylized pictures of the moon and four more that contain that picture as an element of their construction. Good calligraphers often add several more when creating a hanging scroll of the poem, by "deforming" characters and elements that are similar in form to the moon character. The creative imagination finds, in the moon, a celestial connection between separated friends, lovers, or family members.

In China, this is probably the single best-known and best-loved of all classical poems. It is said that in the old days even illiterate peasants could chant the poem by heart.

"Jade Stairs Lament," p. 91: The moon, so important to Li Po, appears again here, captured in and multiplied by the facets of the hanging crystal curtain (its facets speaking in a chorus of potential *togetherness*) as it mocks the spurned lover.

"At Ch'iu-pu Lake," p. 91: This quatrain is from a group of seventeen. Whereas Tu Fu experimented with *chueh chu*, for the most part Li Po just wrote them (and then wrote some more). There is a famous story about this particular one: a young Japanese pupil, having read the poem in an elementary school class, insisted that Li Po was a liar, since no one could have hair three thousand yards long. I wonder how the perhaps apocryphal little boy felt about the line when he saw *his* first white hair?

"Bathing," p. 93: In the first four lines Li Po is in apparent agreement with the arrogance of Ch'u Yuan, but in the last two lines he switches to the mocking voice of "The Fisherman's Song."

"Ancient Air," p. 94: The opening lines of this poem, full of the names of the stars of the sky and of literary history, are only background for one of the few occasions when Li Po allows the cruel realities of his times into the privileged world of his imagination.

"To the Tune of *P'u-sa-man*," p. 96: One of Li Po's many most famous poems, this is an early example of the *tz'u*, a new form of verse discussed in the introduction. Here we find Li Po alluding to poem 13 of the "Nineteen Old Poems of the Han."

"Ruins: The Ku-su Palace," p. 98: This great little poem and the one that follows represent a type of Chinese poem called the *tiao ku*, poems written on historical sites, in most cases ruins, that speak of the ephemeral nature of the worldly glories: *sic transit gloria mundi,* as Thomas à Kempis reminds the popes, in the words of their splendid and glorious inaugural rituals. To my mind, these two little poems by Li Po put Shelley's pillar of Ozymandias in the shade.

"Searching for the Taoist Monk Ch'ang at South Creek," p. 98–99: The phrase "all words gone" is most obviously an echo of T'ao Ch'ien. It originally appears, as François Cheng has pointed out, in Chuang Tzu. Both of these sources were doubtless familiar to the poet.

"Moonlight Night," p. 99: *Longpeace* is the translation of Ch'ang-an, the T'ang capital. I have translated this place name here, because Tu Fu clearly intended its ironic effect.

"Captive Spring," p. 100: As always, Tu Fu's life is a tangle of the personal and the political. He shows perhaps better than any other Chinese poet how completely the two are one for a responsible man of talent. In this poem, isolated, trapped in the rebel-occupied capital, he thinks first of his wife and then of his responsibility as an official. The latter he shows subtly, referring only to the fact that as he wastes his time in the capital his hair is growing too thin to hold the pin that was used to hold his official's cap in place.

"Song of the Bound Chickens," p. 101: One of the reasons Tu Fu is great is that he truly does make ideas (and metaphors and philosophical arguments) *out of things.* Juan Chi and T'ao Ch'ien were intellectuals as well as poets, but they weave their intellectual webs from conventional poetic language. Tu Fu needs just a chicken and an ant to discuss slavery (and slave owning). Thomas Jefferson would certainly have shivered at this poem, or, had he written it, we might find it easier to forgive our greatest leader his trespasses.

"Thinking of My Little Boy," p. 102: This and the next three poems all deal with Tu Fu's sons. There has been a scholarly discussion of whether the first two poems refer to the same son as the second two poems. I think that's irrelevant, and that what is relevant is that Tu Fu loved his sons, and they him. He loved his daughters, too, as other poems of his clearly show.

"Gone by Myself to the Riverbank, in Search of a Flower," pp. 104–106: Here Tu Fu visits a brothel. Showing that to write about such ordinary behavior is not in itself quite so ordinary, he justifies his visit with the none too subtle juxtaposition of the grave of the Buddhist abbot and the house of the madam, the two of whom share the surname Huang, which is, certainly not coincidentally, the color of the earth (*huang* denotes a color that ranges from dark brown to a yellowish tan) in which the abbot lies.

"Thoughts While Traveling by Night," p. 114: The *wen* that is referred to here is the *wen* with so many different related meanings that may be the most important concept separating the modern West from traditional China. It has often been rendered as "letters" or "the written word" in translations of this poem, but I have left it as *wen* to emphasize its greater meaning. Though Tu Fu certainly harbored a desired to be remembered, to attain immortality for his literary works, I am convinced that the "fame" he desired was something (may I say it?) more noble than fame for a talent, even one developed into a surpassing skill, a sublime art. A thoroughgoing Confucian (though clearly the sort of epicurean we call a Taoist and certainly the most humane sort of T'ien-T'ai Buddhist as well) such as Tu Fu wanted fame for having achieved *wen*, for deserving to be called a *chun tzu*, a just and humane governor of his community.

"Gazing from High," p. 114: With a series of fairly erudite allusions, Ch'ien Ch'i appears to be telling the monks (true men) that though his heart is with them he cannot perform miracles (like Bodhidharma crossing the river on a reed) to aid them. Most Zen poets avoid literary allusions. Maybe the monks' need overrode Ch'ien Ch'i's observance of Zen poetic convention.

"The Master of Hsiang Plays His Lute," p. 115: *Wu-t'ung* is the catalpa tree, whose large leaves murmur dolefully in a breeze. The scene is the site of Ch'u Yuan's supposed suicide.

"Song of the South of the River," p. 116: As often happens with a translation, the most interesting action happens offstage in the realm of the untranslatable: the wave riders are young men (with all the panache and romantic cachet of our own surfers) who ride the tidal bore, the annual tidal wave that runs up the Yangtze for phenomenal distances inland. These tough guys surpass the trader/traitor husband ironically in regularity of visit (at least once a year) and also perhaps in sexual attractiveness: so the translator has the traveling salesman's wife cry something along the lines of "I shoulda married a surfer."

"Moored at Maple Bridge," p. 117: This great quatrain hangs, in calligraphic form, on the walls of tens of millions of homes and offices today. The poet sees the sadness in the chaos inevitably attendant upon the fall of a dynasty. The temple bell offers solace, even a reminder of the possibility of salvation, to every traveler. To show this in English required more than four lines.

"Grass on the Ancient Plain," p. 118: It is likely that Po Chu-i intended to give this little farewell a political twist. The grass, "tender" as a friendship, and tough as a true one as well, may also be meant to stand for "the people," whose welfare was the shared moral and ethical goal of Po Chu-i and his here unnamed friend.

"The Charcoal Man," p. 119: This poem is a perfect example of the sort of political poetry that won Po Chu-i fame as an upstanding supporter of social justice in the best Confucian tradition. Along with his close friend, the poet Yuan Chen, he is credited with creating a new genre of socially critical poetry, called the Hsin Yueh Fu, or New Music Bureau Poems. However, the reader is sure to notice the similarity between "The Charcoal Man," and

Tu Fu's "The Press-Gang at Shih-hao Village," (pp. 110–111), a poem written more than a century earlier.

"The Old Fisherman," p. 120: Liu Tsung-yuan, renowned through Chinese history as both a poet and a prose master, was also a Buddhist politician who was involved in a constantly fluctuating battle for control of the late T'ang court. The references in this famous poem to the state of Ch'u and the River Hsiang (where Ch'u Yuan was said to have drowned himself) and to the Ch'u period poem "The Fisherman's Song" clearly show that Liu intended us to travel back with him a thousand years from his time to forge our understanding of his ethical, spiritual, and political position here. Can we suppose that he would allow us to rest a little first, after our 1,200-year trip to his late T'ang?

"River Snow," p. 120: This is one of the most famous of all the great T'ang dynasty quatrains. Your acquaintance with Ch'u Yuan and his fisherman friend is not the key to a cipher: a poem is not (usually) written in code. But your knowledge may deepen the mysterious beauty that has allowed this poem to live nearly a dozen centuries so far.

"Searching, and Not Finding, the Hermit," p. 120: *Simples* refers to medicinal herbs.

"Passing the Night in a Village Inn," p. 121: In addition to the two poems included here for this poet under his secular name, Chia Tao, several more are included in the T'ang Zen section under his "name in religion," Wu Pen, by which he was known during the early part of his life when a shaven-headed Zen Buddhist monk.

"Don't Go Out, Sir!" pp. 121–122: Perhaps his own poor health caused Li Ho to identify with Confucius's favorite disciple, Yen Hui, who also died young. Readers who imagine that Taoism and Buddhism are the sources of all wildly imaginative literature and literary figures in China should take note that mad as he is, Li Ho still knows that Confucian belief is at the core of the Chinese cultural experience. Besides Yen Hui, several other Confucian exemplars are mentioned in the poem, and the reference to the wearing of orchids is an allusion to Ch'u Yuan himself.

"The Tomb of Su Hsiao-hsiao," p. 122: Su Hsiao-hsiao is the name of a famous courtesan. Here, at its most restrained, Li Ho's style certainly still has a ghostly power.

"Confession," p. 122: Here, "won a name" is a ferociously ironic pun: to win a name means to gain fame in Chinese, just as in English, though certainly the distinction between (honorable) fame and infamy or notoriety was clearer in Tu Mu's time than in our own even in China. Chiang-nan is China's scenic sunny south. *Yang-chou dreams* refers to illusory dreams of luxury.

"Untitled," by Li Shang-yin, p. 124: It's generally agreed that the explanation for the abstruse quality of Li Shang-yin's poems lies primarily in the fact that they are artifacts of the processes of courtly sexual intrigues: that is, he's both angling for lovers, attempting to communicate with them, and bragging of his conquests. The quality of the language and the gossip surrounding the subject matter have kept him ranked high in popularity among lovers of T'ang poetry. Some readers would say these two poems are not a fair sample. I think they are.

PART FOUR: *A Few Strong Voices Still Singing*

The Poetry of Ou-yang Hsiu, pp. 160–164: This selection includes six *tz'u* poems and six classical quatrains. Ou-yang Hsiu legitimized the *tz'u* as a form by simply signing his culturally very potent name to his poems. Many Sung dynasty poets were writing *tz'u* by his time, but in the conservative culture of the time they were waiting for someone like Ou-yang to make the first step. And he did, in spite of the fact that he was associated with the most conservative of the Confucian political "party." The first group that he published under his own name, two of which are included here, are actually written to a tune title with regular seven-syllable lines, so the innovator cheated just a little, not going all the way here, as he did later, to the irregular line length that was the real mark of the *tz'u*.

"A painted skiff," p. 162: This and the next poem are taken from Ou-yang's groundbreaking first set of nonanonymous *tz'u*. They are all excellent poems in their own right. The repeated "West Lake's good" uses the simplest word for "good" in the Chinese language, obviously intentionally. Thus Ou-yang beat Ernest Hemingway to the punch by about nine centuries. In the poem above he puns on the word for "to hold office," which also means to "endure." As the two poems suggest, Ou-yang Hsiu was in (somewhat less than rigorous) political exile when he wrote this set of "radical" poems.

"Face turned to falling flowers; a breeze, ripples on the water," p. 163: Among the many little superstitions common among the Chinese (like our knocking on wood after speaking wishfully, or saying "gesundheit" or "bless you" after a sneeze) is the prohibition regarding the sharing of a pear by lovers or a married couple. It is based on the fact that the pear is called *li* in Chinese and to divide (share) is pronounced "fen." *Fenli*, pronounced the same but not written with the same characters, means "to separate," and so the sharing of a pear between loved ones is forbidden. (If only it were so easy to do away with separation.) The translator's play at the end of this poem is based on a similar play on the part of Ou-yang.

"Two Poems on Paintings by Mr. Yin," p. 166: Here the toad and the snail may refer to specific political and social climbers probably well known to the poet's audience. No insult to real toads and snails, living or dead, is intended, I am sure.

"To the Abbot of the Tung-lin Monastery," p. 167: This quatrain is often identified as Su Shih's "enlightenment poem," it being traditional for clerical and lay practitioners of Zen alike to compose a poem (a *gatha*, or hymn of praise) when they first experienced spiritual awakening. That the last line should seem something of a challenge to the abbot does not necessarily disqualify this poem as an expression of enlightenment. The reference to the Buddha in the first two lines is oblique but unmistakable.

"Four Verses," p. 187–189: Chang Yang-hao is a fascinating character, maybe because in the final analysis his answer to his own apparently rhetorical question here was a surprisingly nonrhetorical "yes." He served the government early in life in an official capacity, but was early forced to flee the capital in disguise as a result of a penchant for honest advice. When he was called back to service, asked to take over government of an area under siege by famine, he did not falter from the Confucian ideal of service, and he died in office, it is said, of overwork.

"Ching-wei," p. 206: The *ching-wei* is a mythical bird, one that, in mythical, prehistoric times, tried to fill up the sea with pebbles to express her loyalty. Ku Yen-wu sees himself as a "modern-day" *ching-wei*, a Sisyphus condemned by his own sense of honor to fight the Manchus one pebble at a time, while, as the end of the poem suggests, birds of another feather are building and feathering their own nests. This is one of the least opaque of Ku's poems.

"Eight Feet," pp. 206–207: There is an allusion in almost every line of this poem. The feeling of mystery that I hope this translation may hint at would have inspired the poem's contemporary reader to attempt to decipher its literary code. That attempt, using reference works like the immense dictionary of poetic phrases called the *P'ei-wen Yun-fu* to supplement the monumental amount of material held in memory by the conventionally trained Confucian reader, still wouldn't have been easy. The ordinary literate person, the audience for the poems of a Yuan Mei, a Ching An, or a Su Man-shu, and of China's then rapidly growing body of really excellent colloquial fiction, probably wouldn't have been either interested in or able to master the task.

"Talking Art," p. 207: In a fairly rare foray into "critical discourse," Yuan Mei brings the most radical contemporary artistic critical theory straight into play (playfully, to be sure) in inimitable style, as he applies it to poetry.

"So Be It," p. 208: The moss in the path has been growing since the earliest Chinese poems. Yuan Mei is surely thinking back, here, to the moss growing in Li Po's famous "Ballad of Ch'ang-kan." The poetic tradition is reflected on Yuan Mei's gown in the poem at hand.

"Ginseng," p. 208–209: A preference for invigorating ginseng over long-winded philosophizing provides a succinct critique of the mean-spirited, puritanical, nitpicking fundamentalism that Chu Hsi's neo-Confucianism had become in the hands of the Chinese who were Manchu collaborationists.

"Speaking My Mind," p. 209: Ou-yang Hsiu's "Lang-ye Creek" is more elegant, but Yuan Mei's broad, almost Monty Python–style humor is more suited to a democratized "Wang Yang-ming-ist," anti-Manchu middle-class audience. It represents a classical style that could conceivably become part of the repertoire of modern Chinese poets.

"Late Gazing," p. 210–211: Despite his (misplaced) reputation as anti-Buddhist, here, as in the next poem, "The Bell," Yuan Mei points to Buddhism as the source of needed radical change in the Chinese polity as well as in poetry. Yuan Mei's favorite Confucian, the radical democrat Wang Yang-ming, was condemned in his own time by Chu Hsi-ists as a crypto-Zenist.

"Gone Again to Gaze on the Cascade," p. 212: Wei-ma (in Sanskrit, Vimalakirti) was a lay disciple of the historical Buddha who confounded a conclave of monks by answering a fundamental metaphysical question with "a thunderous silence." Wei-ma was a favorite of Chinese literary folk partly for his refusal to enter into arguments (à la Chuang Tzu) and partly because he remained a layman. Yuan Mei's reference to T'ao Ch'ien (specifically to his "Drinking Wine," number 5) is brilliantly silly, the epitome of Yuan Mei's genius. Note that it is also another reprise of Ou-yang Hsiu's "Lang-ye Creek."

"Finished with a Long Parting Poem," pp. 213–214: Clearly the *Shih Ching (The Poetry Classic)* is with Yuan Mei and with his audience.

"In Idleness," p. 213: Yuan Mei was finally set aside by the Manchu rulers who found him, in his clearly intentional failure of a mandatory Manchu language examination, simply too arrogant to rise any higher, whatever his other manifest talents. I'm inclined to accept his willingness to "lead" his family into the utopian kingdom of his retirement as only humorously self-mocking rather than deeply bitter. Fame, prestige, and power might be hard to turn down, but so was the free life of a popular poet. People were literally singing his praises in the streets of Nanjing and making his variety of works in both verse and prose best sellers in the booksellers' stalls.

"Ah Chen," p. 214: In traditional China, fathers seldom wrote poems for their daughters. Yuan Mei loved his children, and he is proud of the dangerously unconventional upbringing he and his wife have given their daughter. Their only care was where to find a man with the courage and understanding to marry an educated woman.

"Dusk of Autumn," p. 220: "What my heart embraces": yes, indeed, directly connecting this twentieth-century poet to Juan Chi, whose "book" was, as you doubtless recall, "Sing of what my heart embraces." The part of his monk's oath that he's referring to is the part that would stop him writing poems. Fat chance. Rules are made . . .

"Beating the Heat at Jade Lake," p. 221: In a widely praised poem, not included here, Ching An refers to himself as "worn-out sandals" facing the emperor. Chang An's figure (representing himself as an empty robe, not as a man) is creative even though it was certainly consciously made in homage to Tu Fu. More than a thousand years and less than a synapse separate these two great poets of the great tradition.

"Moored at Maple Bridge," p. 222: This is, of course, the same Maple Bridge that Chang Chi made famous in the T'ang. How dare a Zen master suffer so? In the 1980s Gary Snyder published a poem in *The New Yorker* about a visit there, crossing space (and cultural boundaries) as well as time.

"Laughing at Myself, I," pp. 222–223: Many a Zen-inspired writer, beginning in the T'ang with the monk Chiao Jan and the layman Po Chu-i, wrote of trying to give up poetry. Yuan Mei shares an animus for the inventor of writing, but as a bibliophile rather than as a writer.

"Laughing at Myself, II," p. 223: In a not totally unusual display of piety, as a young man Ching An burned off two of his fingers earning himself the lifelong nickname Pa-chih T'ou-t'uo, "the eight-fingered monk." In an insightful moment later in life he wrote this very nice poem, which might serve as a useful reminder to all about the wisdom of age, or maybe the unwisdom of youth, precisely to those aforesaid youth who might admire and wish to emulate the Old Guy in too many ways.

"Passing the Birthplace of Cheng Ch'eng-kung's Last Loyal Defender of the Ming," p. 224: Here again, Tu Fu's straw sandals, Ching An's empty robe. No reader would miss the mixture of pride and humility in the reuse of this honored figure.

"Random Verses, I," p. 225: The likening of the flood refugees to geese comes straight from the *Shih Ching*; stranded fish, more artfully, from Chuang Tzu. The poet is probably not trying to cast aspersions on specific political rivals here, but rather simply to show how important good government is to all the people, when it comes to practical affairs. (The maintenance of elaborate irrigation and flood control of both the Yellow River and Yangtze valleys was one of the most obvious of these sacred—and practical—duties of government.)

"Random Verses, II," p. 225–226: Newly married and traveling with his bride, Tseng lets "popular Taoism" with its varieties of magical tricks and "recreational" meditation into his poem . . . only deep mind meditation, and the silliness of Chuang Tzu, an approved classical philosopher for all his whimsy, pass muster in a classical poem for most poets in the musty Ch'ing.